How to Draw Anime Characters in 13 Steps or Less!

Stephanie Lane

Table of Contents

Disclaimer

While all attempts have been made to verify the information provided in this book, the author does assume any responsibility for errors, omissions, or contrary interpretations of the subject matter contained within. The information provided in this book is for educational and entertainment purposes only. The reader is responsible for his or her own actions and the author does not accept any responsibilities for any liabilities or damages, real or perceived, resulting from the use of this information.

The trademarks that are used are without any consent, and the publication of the trademark is without permission or backing by the trademark owner. All trademarks and brands within this book are for clarifying purposes only and are the owned by the owners themselves, not affiliated with this document.

Introduction

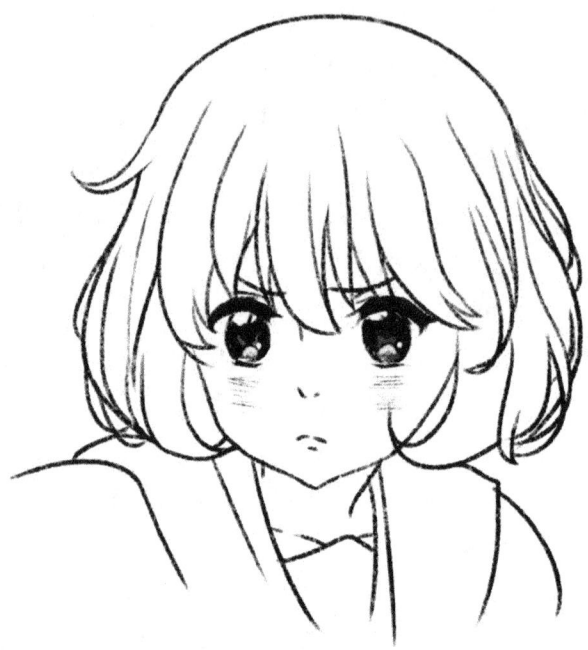

Beginning in 1917 with the release of Dekobo Shingacho-Meian no Shippai, anime has continued to grow as a popular stylized art form with some films in this genre grossing over 200 million dollars! Successful shows in this genre have achieved even higher earnings, reaching grosses into the billions.

Like any other art form, learning to draw anime takes time and practice, but thankfully there are distinct characteristics seen in anime drawings that are easy to master and will be explained in this book. So, by following the guided steps provided, you should be well on your way to mastering the art of anime!

Part 1: Front Faces

Judgemental Boy

1. Create an arc similar to the letter "C" to form the outline for the hair:

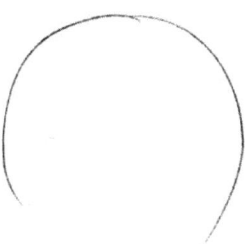

2. Mark feature lines for the eyes, eyebrows, nose, and mouth. Create the jaw by forming to slanted lines that converge under the lip to form a point:

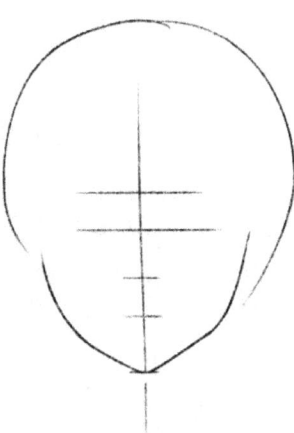

3. Draw two lines to form the neck. Draw two squares and connect them to the neck. Create lines that form a "V" shape to make the collar:

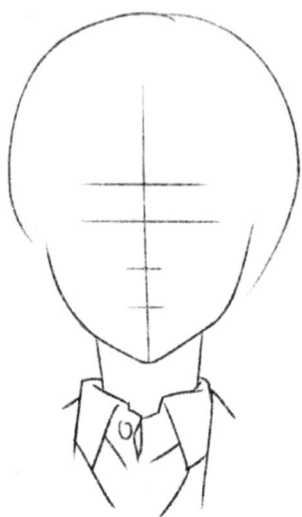

4. Draw lines like semi-circles to form ears. Add "V" shaped lines and some arcs to contour the hair:

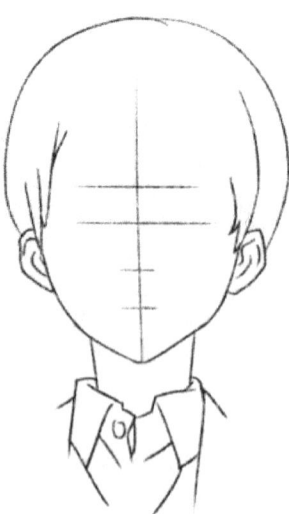

5. Draw sharp lines ending in points to create hair:

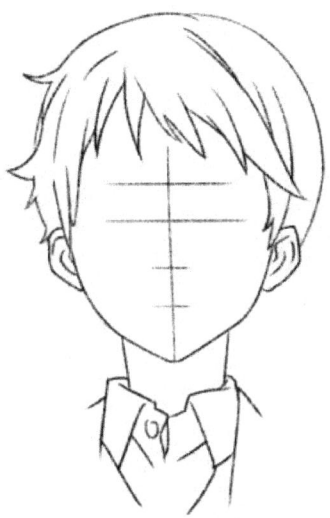

6. Add more sharp points to develop the hair. Draw two small lines and a dot to form the nose:

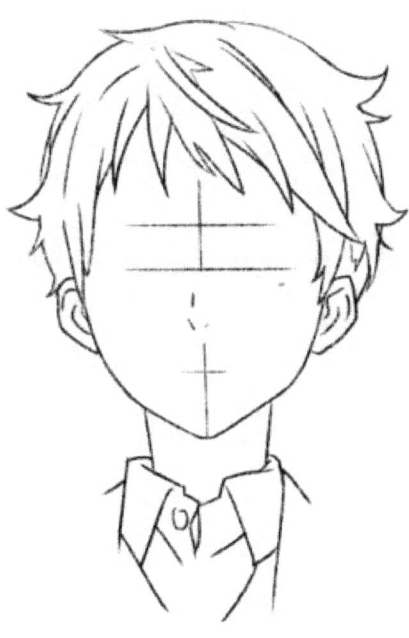

7. Draw an arc with a tiny line under it to make the mouth:

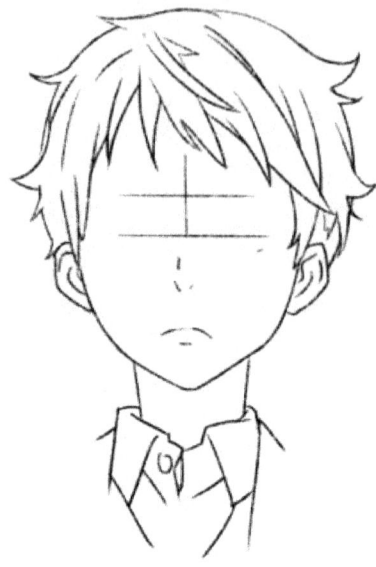

8. Form almond shapes for the eyes. Make small slits for eyelashes:

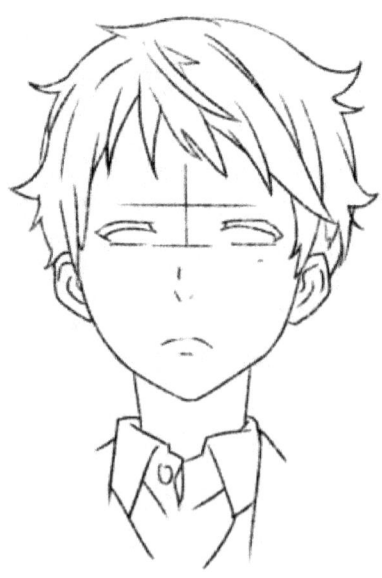

9. Shade in the irises and leave a white dot for the pupil:

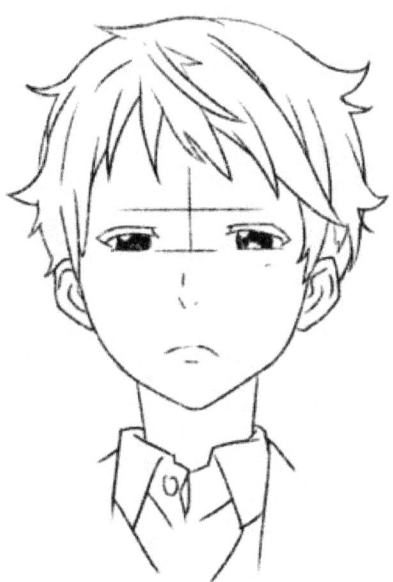

10. Shade in the eyelashes and draw thick dark lines to create eyebrows:

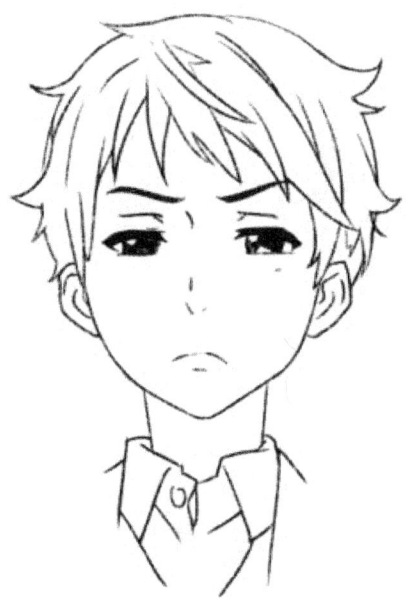

Sad Girl

1. Create a small arc for the outline of the hair:

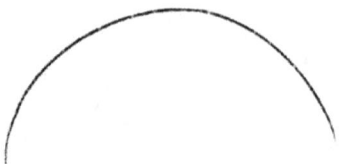

2. Add two more lines to complete the outline of the hair. Make a wide "V" shape to form the jaw:

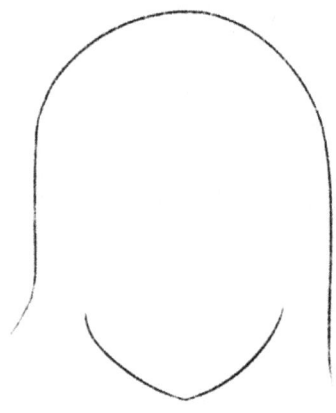

3. Add a straight line in the center of the face to divide it in two. Draw rectangle and "V" shapes to create clothing:

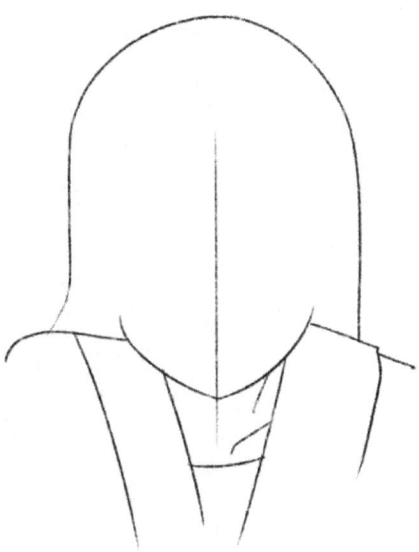

4. Create thin sharp lines to make hair:

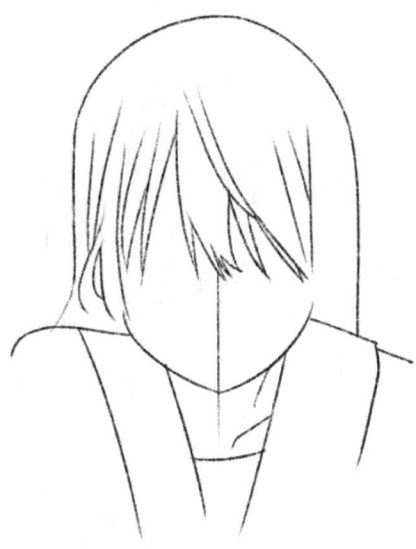

5. Form a small circle with little dots under it to create the nose:

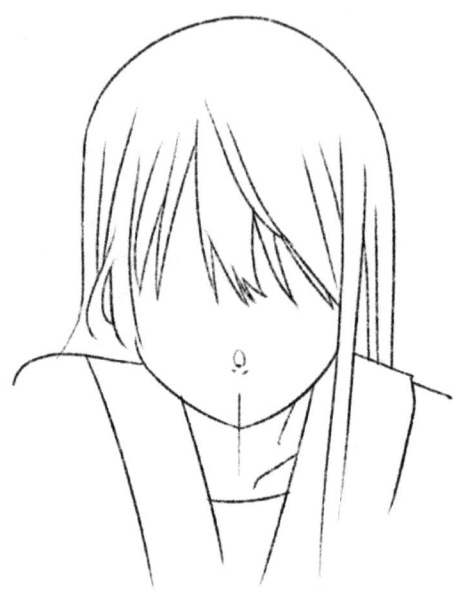

6. Use oval shapes to make ears. Draw two small light lines to create the mouth:

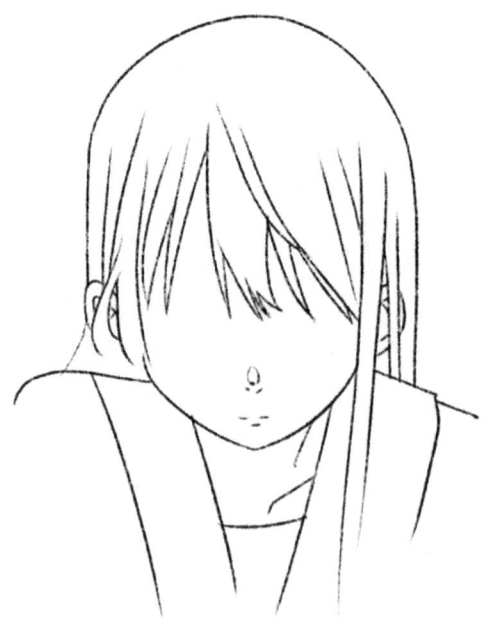

7. Draw guide lines across the face for the eyes and eyebrows:

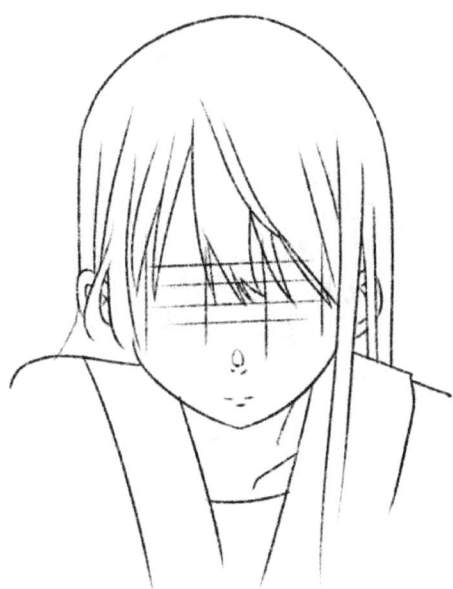

8. Using the lower two guidelines, form thick lines for the eyelashes and thin lines for the eyes:

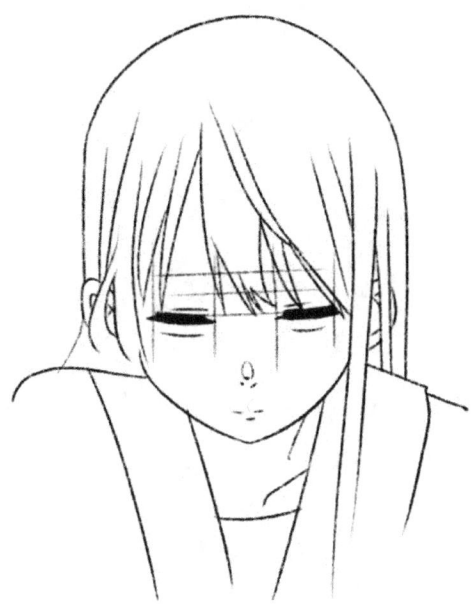

9. Using the two upper guidelines, form small arcs for the eyelids and draw thin lines to make eyebrows. Shade in the eyes:

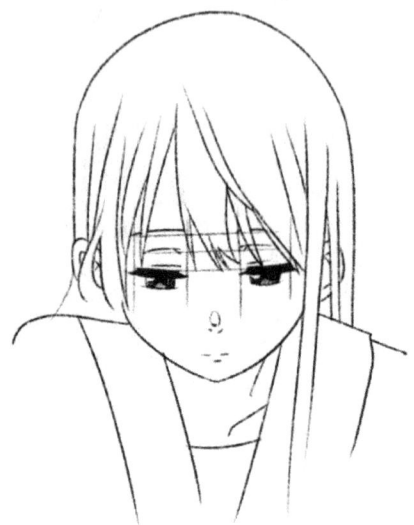

10. Draw rectangle shapes to form the hand and the arm. Use cylinder shapes to make the jacket sleeve:

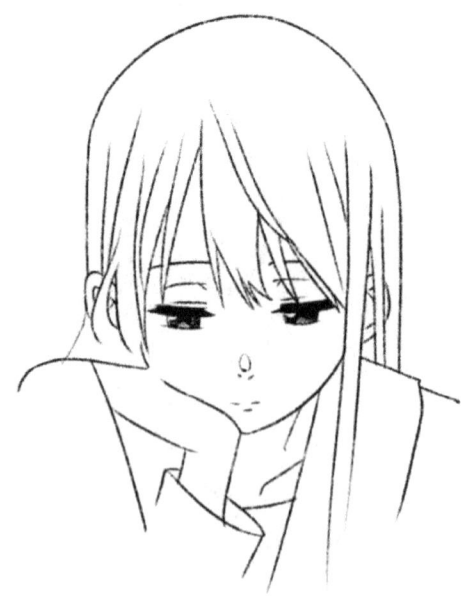

11. Add lines to create fingers. Contour the hand:

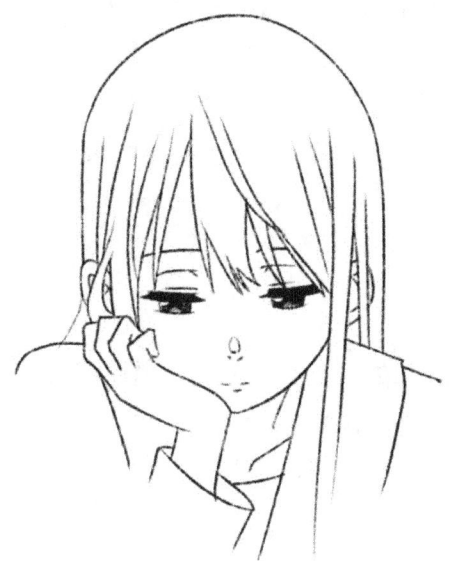

12. Add clover shapes and lines on the top of the hair for highlights. Add a small circle to make a button on the sleeve:

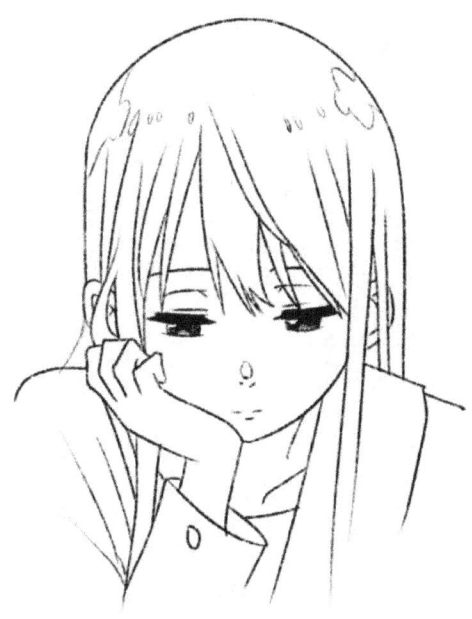

Smug Boy

1. Create an arc similar to the letter "C" to form the hair outline:

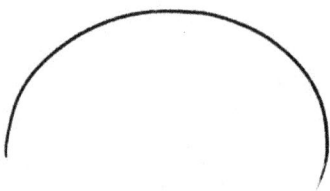

2. Form a line on the right side to outline the face. Create the jaw, leaving a small space for an ear:

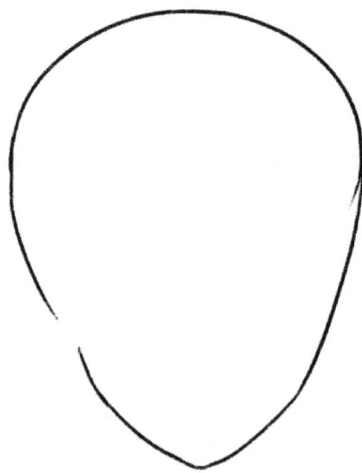

3. Split the face. Draw lines to create shoulders. Draw trapezium and "V" shapes to create a collar and tie:

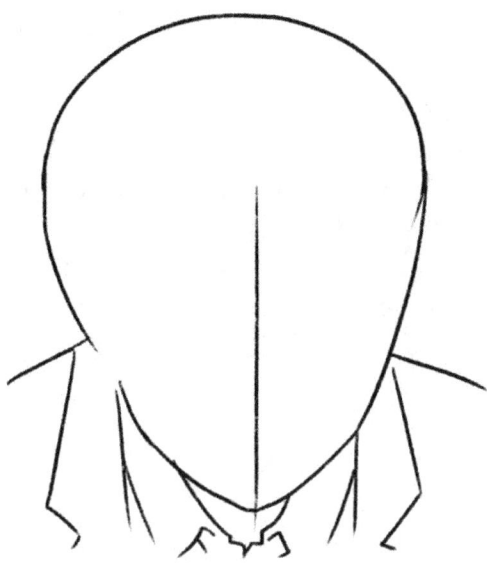

4. Form the ears using wide "v" shapes and curved lines:

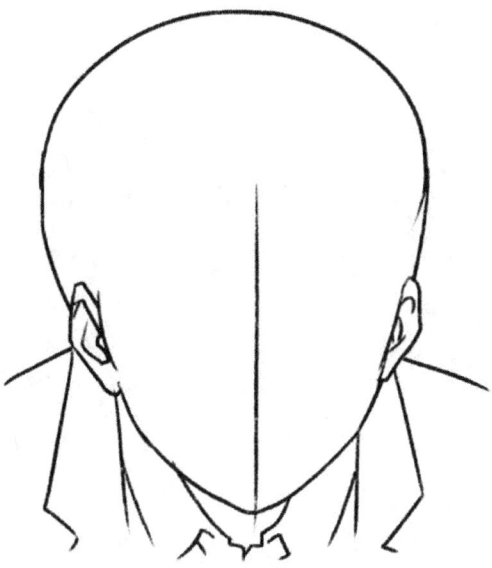

5. Draw several spiky lines to form hair:

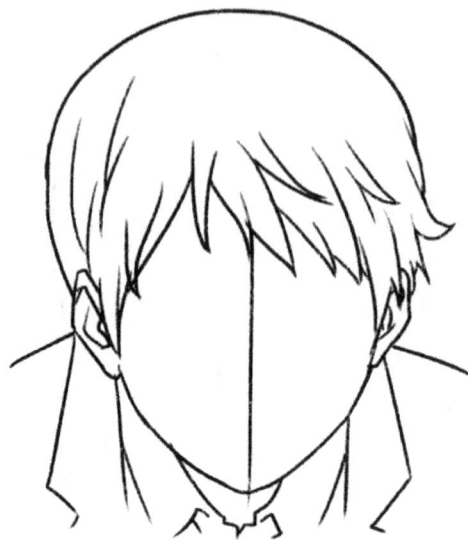

6. Add more sharps lines and steep arcs to give the hair more detail:

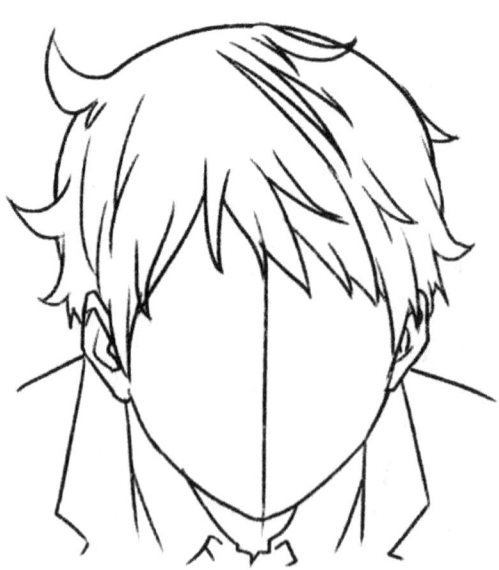

7. Create 3 lines on the face to form guidelines for the eyes and eyebrows:

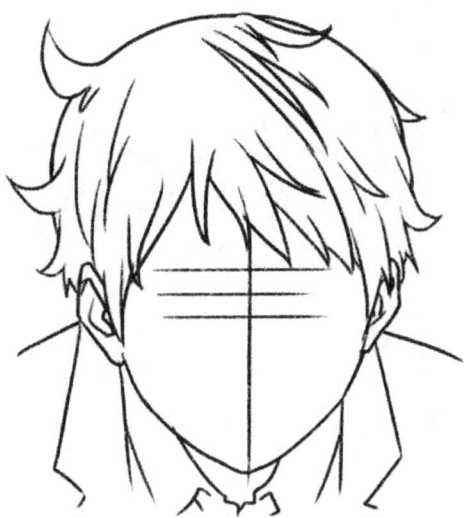

8. Add two more small lines in the lower quarter of the face to make guidelines for the nose and mouth:

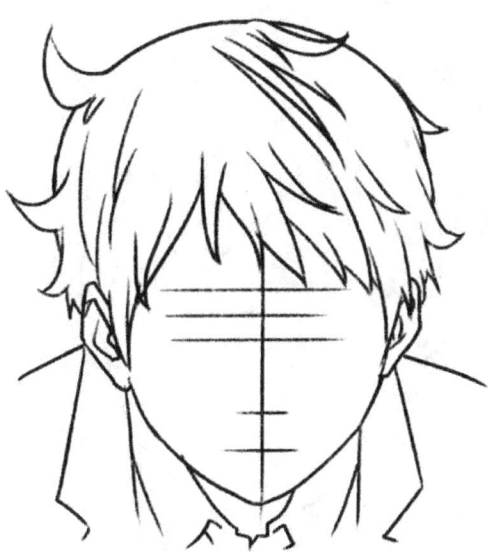

9. Use small lines and arcs to form the nose:

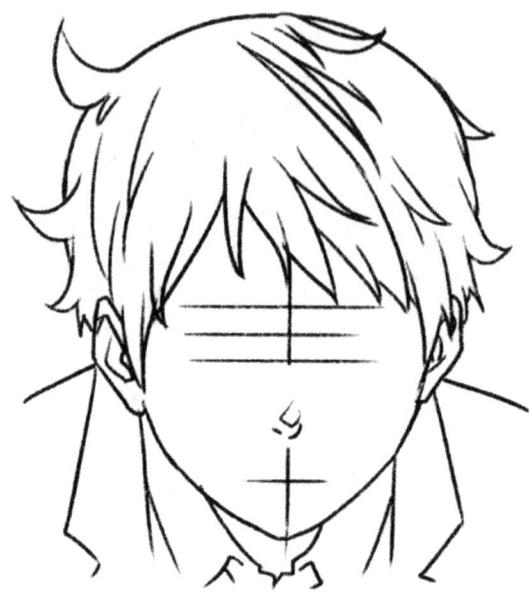

10. Add small lines to form the mouth:

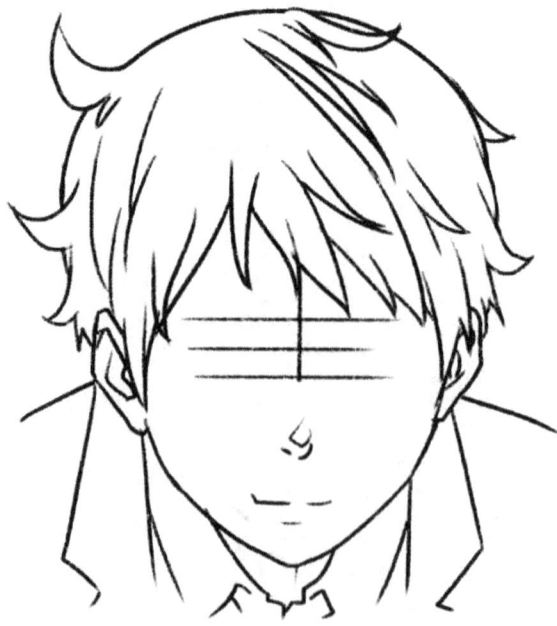

11. Using the bottom two guidelines, draw almond shapes to form eyes:

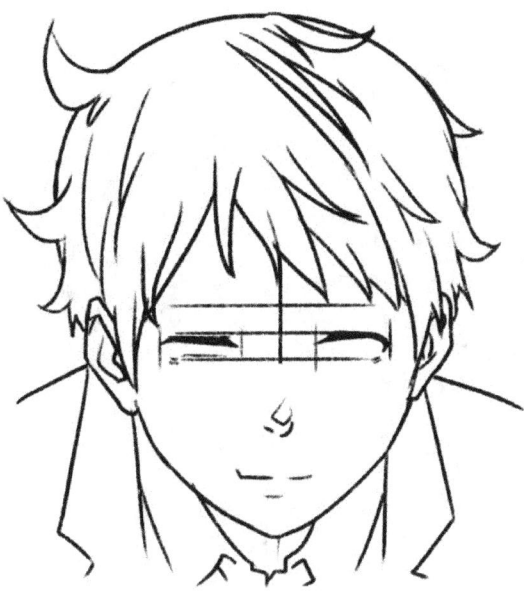

12. Draw circles to make pupils and irises. Draw thick lines to form eyelids:

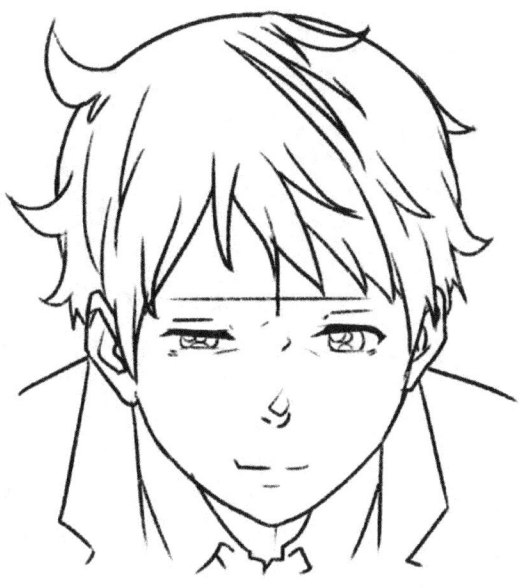

13. Shade in the eyes and draw thick lines to create eyebrows:

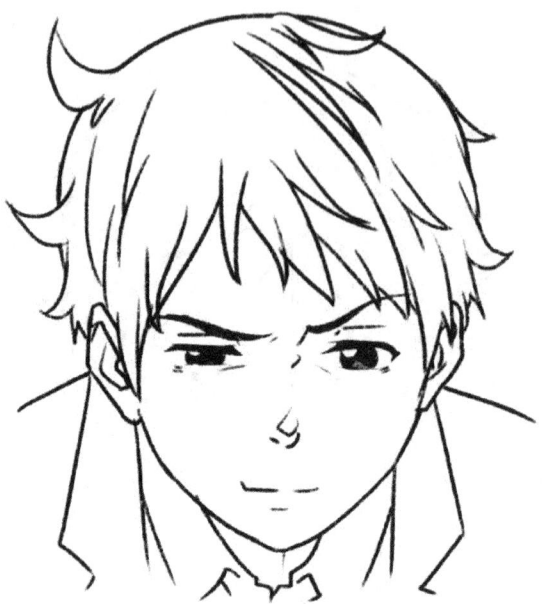

Smirking Teen Boy

1. Draw a "C" shape to outline the hair:

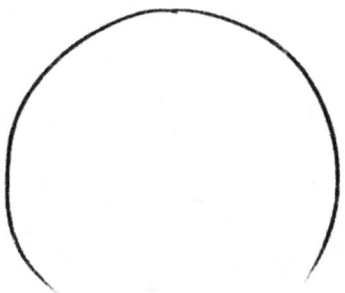

2. Draw a "V" shape to make a face:

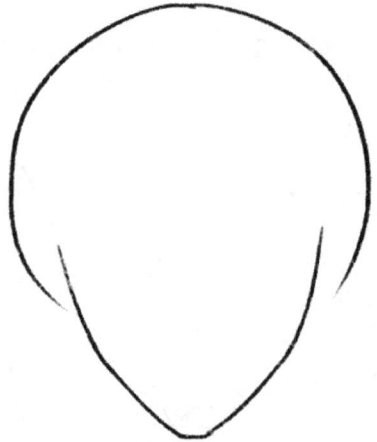

3. Draw guidelines for the facial features:

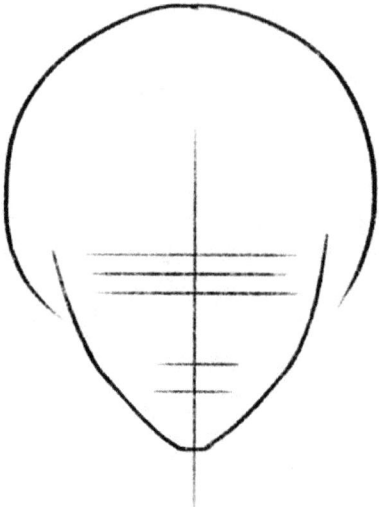

4. Draw pointed lines and small arcs to make ears:

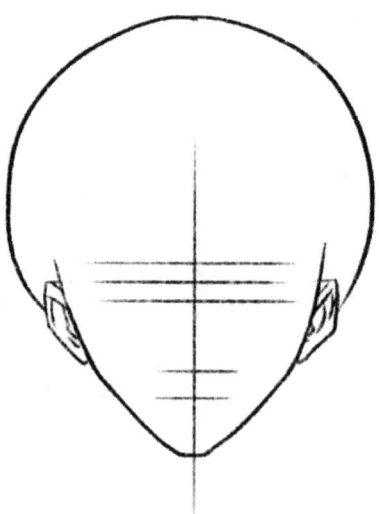

5. Starting on the left side, draw sharp lines to begin creating hair:

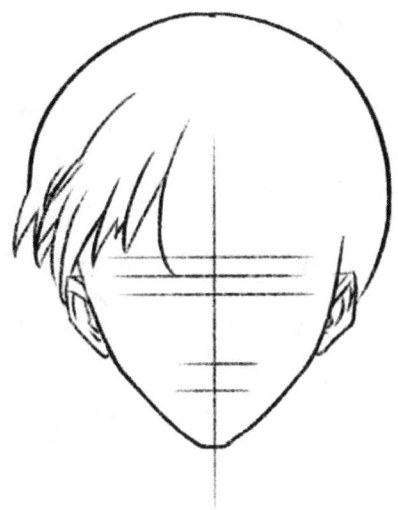

6. Add more points and lines to finish the hair:

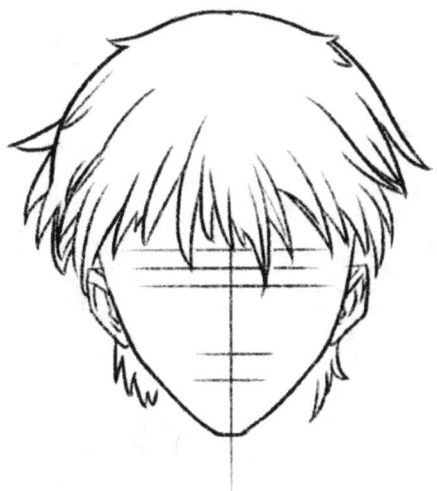

7. Add lines to form the neck and shoulders:

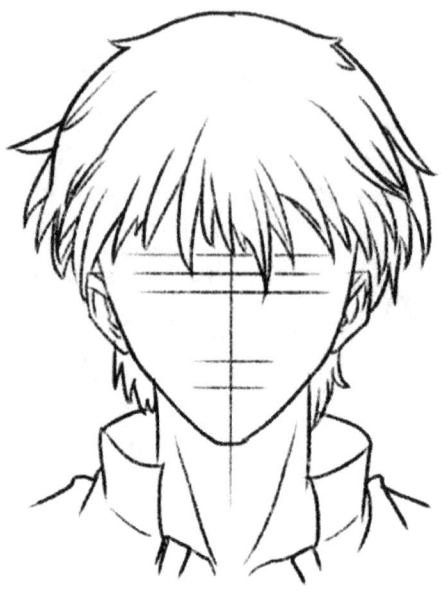

8. Use sharp almond like shapes to make eyes:

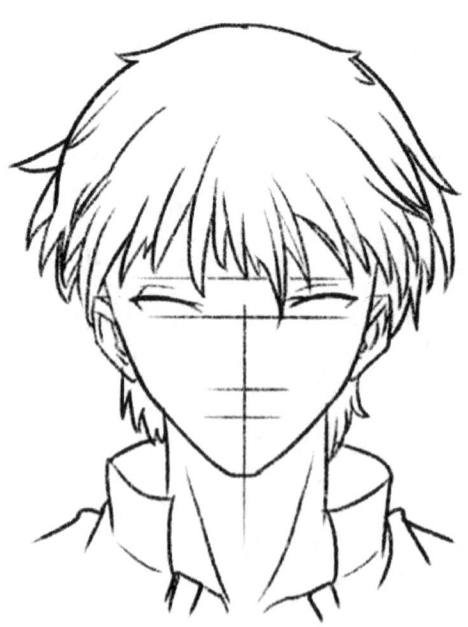

9. Draw hard lines for the eyebrows:

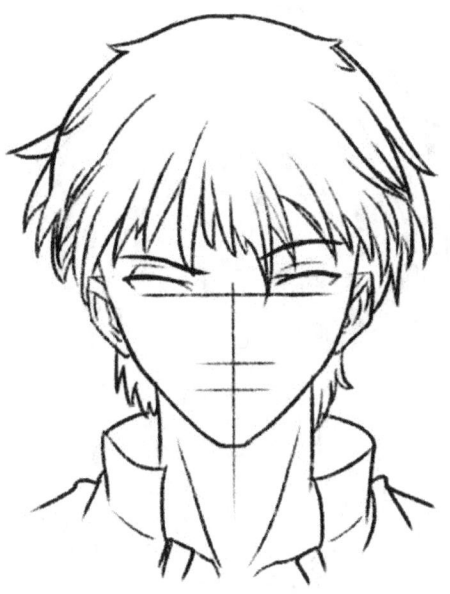

10. Add small lines for the nose and mouth:

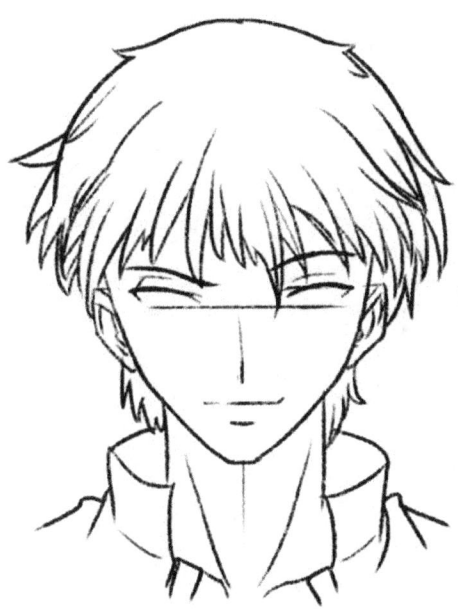

11. Add thick lines for eyelashes and draw circles to make eyes:

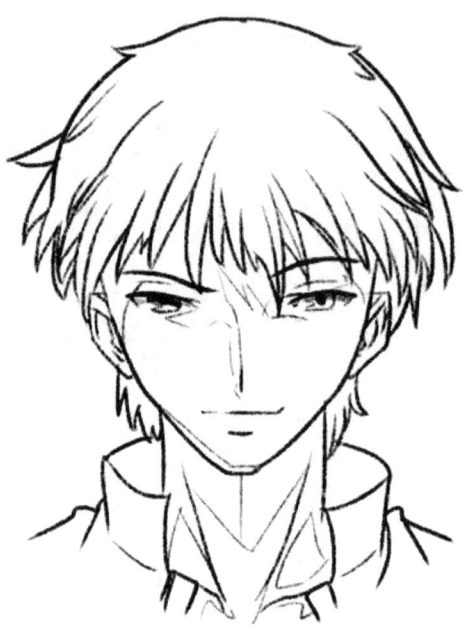

Part 2: ¾ Faces

Depressed Girl

1. Draw an arc to create the hair outline:

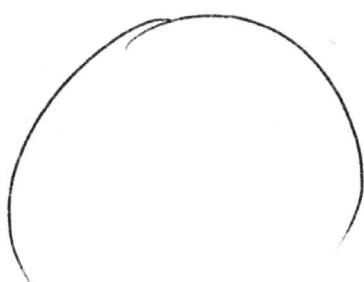

2. Draw lines for the face, and then draw a line down the center:

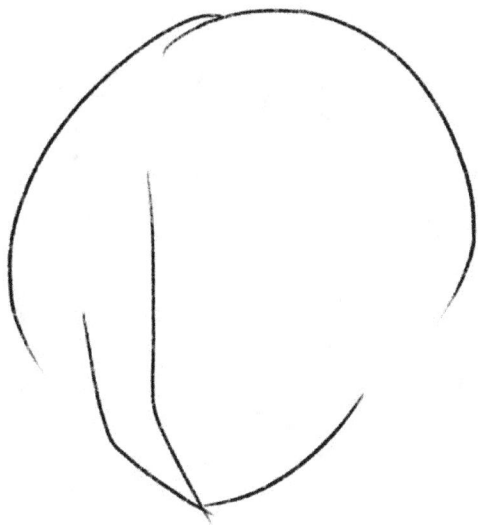

3. Add two guidelines for the eyes:

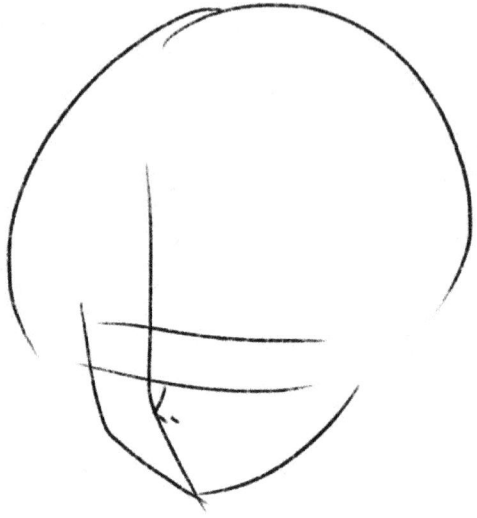

4. Make a small line to create the mouth:

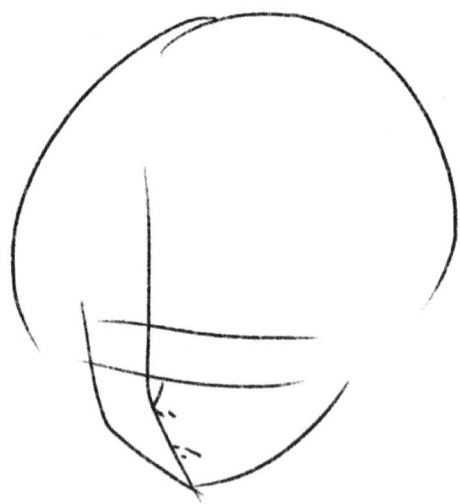

5. Draw to thick lines for eyelashes just below the first guideline:

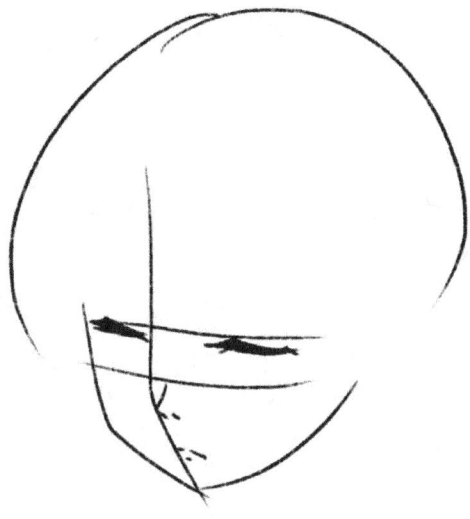

6. Draw to small circles to make eyes:

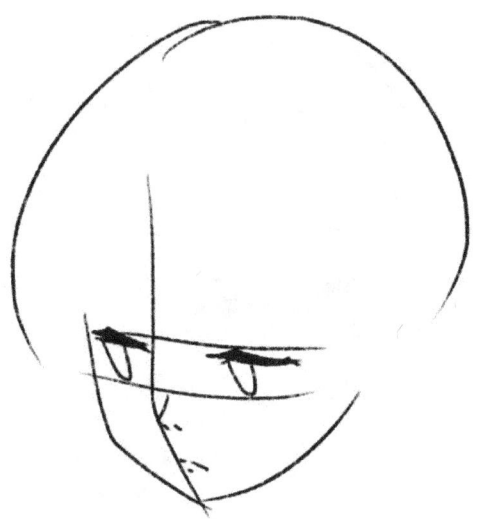

7. Draw lines to makes eyelids and eyebrows:

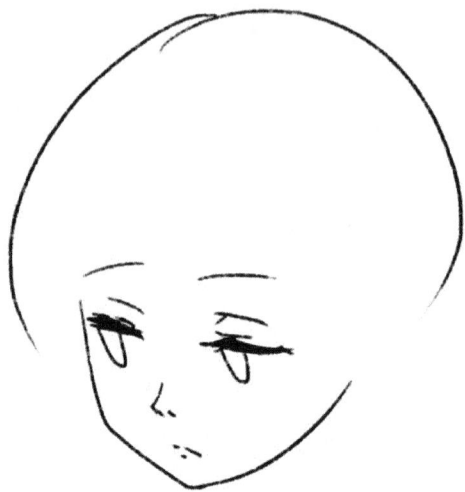

8. Shade in the eyes. Draw lines to make the neck:

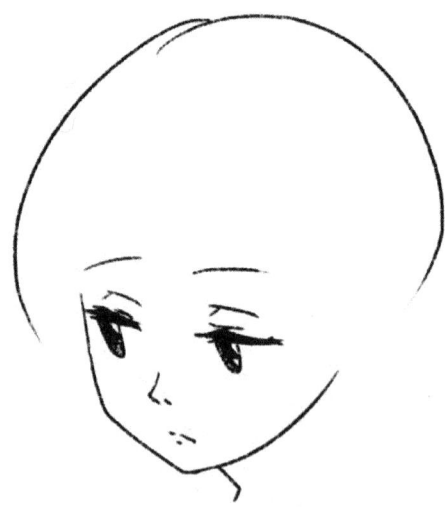

9. Contour the hair shape. Add arcs for shoulders:

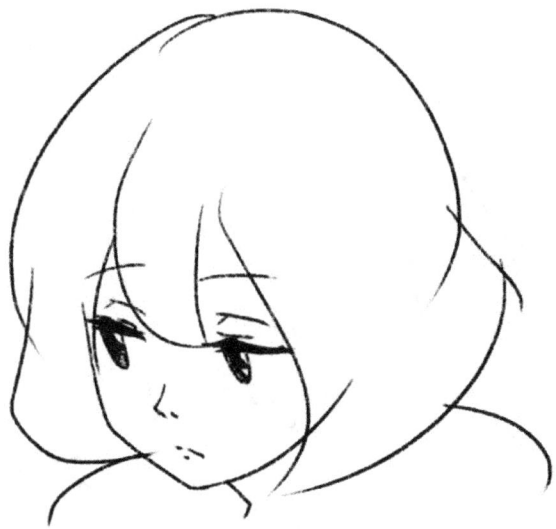

10. Add lines and points to add details to the hair:

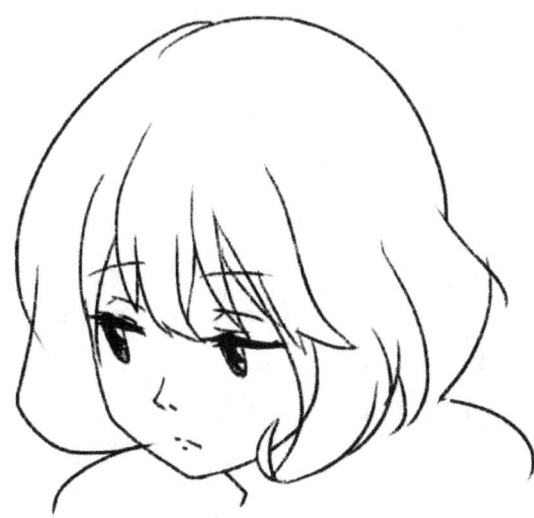

11. Add rectangle shapes to create dress straps. Add more lines to the hair:

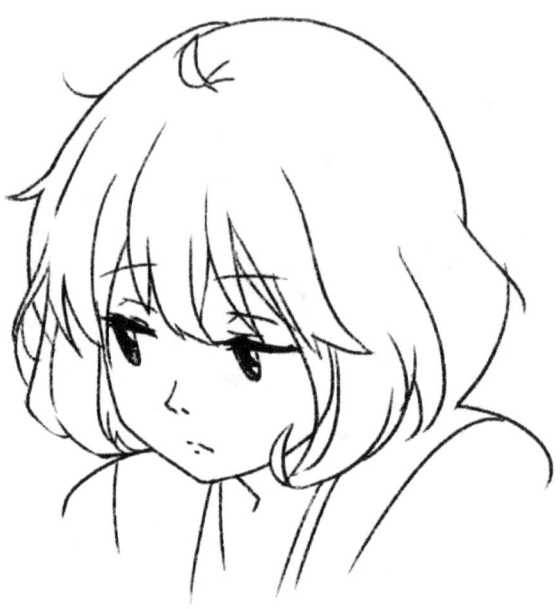

12. Add more lines and points to finish the hair:

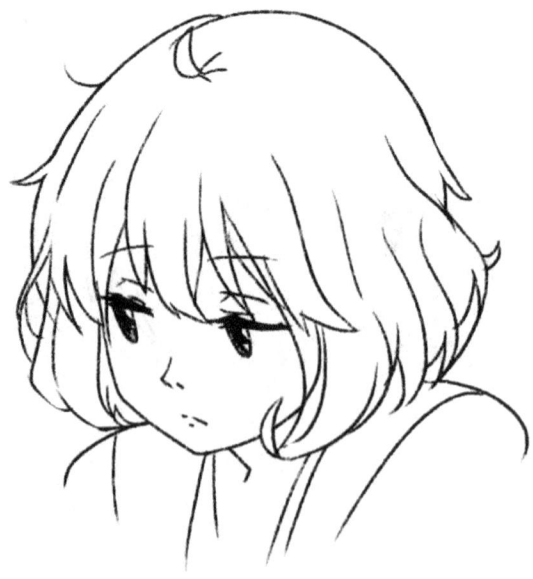

13. Add a series of small lines on each cheek to make blush marks:

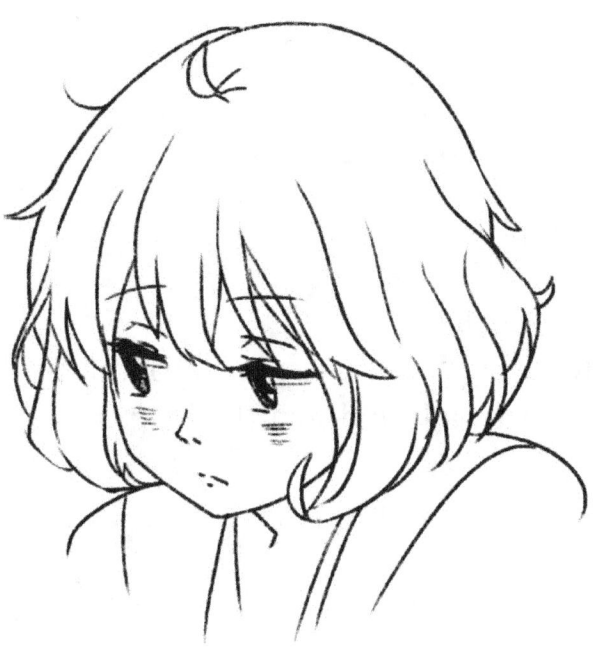

Scared Boy

1. Draw a "C" shape to outline the hair:

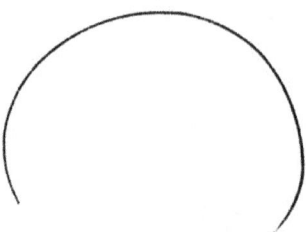

2. Draw two lines ending in a point to make the face leaving space for an ear. Draw a line down the center of the face:

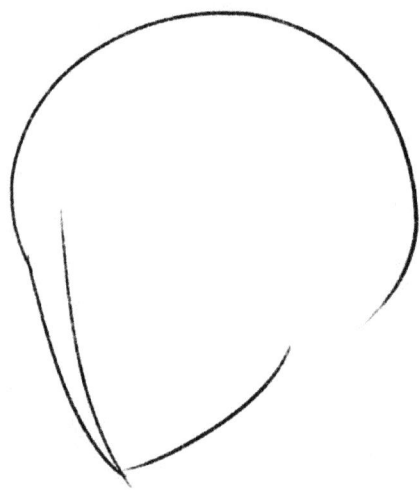

3. Draw guidelines for facial features:

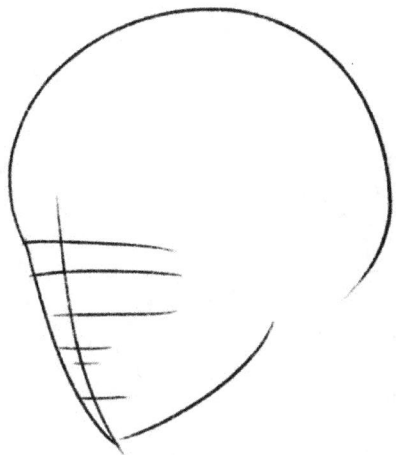

4. Draw sharp lines to begin the hair. Use arcs and an oval shape to make the ear:

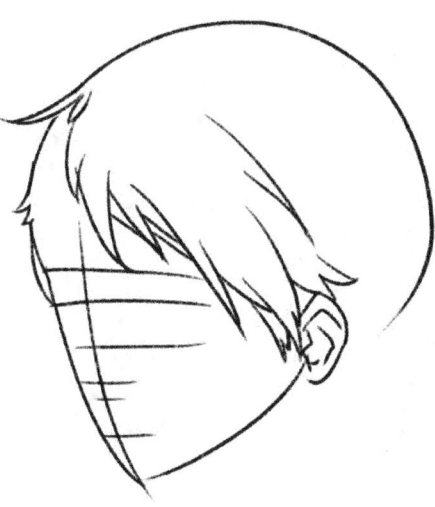

5. Add more serrated lines and points to finish detailing the hair:

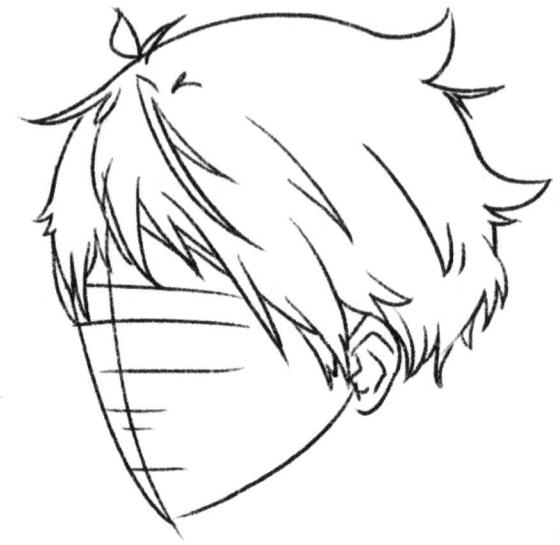

6. Contour the middle of the face to create the forehead:

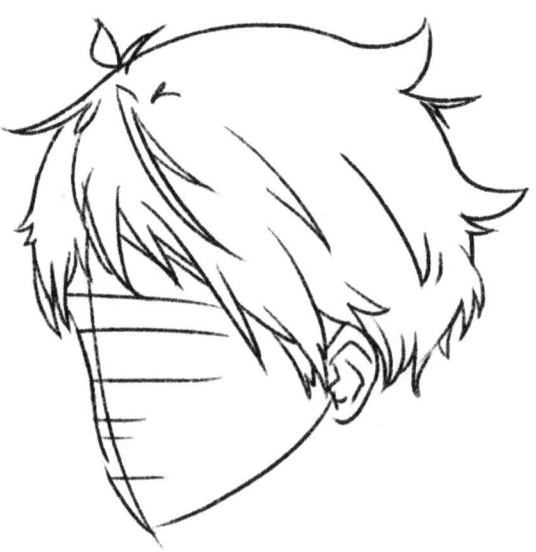

7. Draw the outline of the nose. Draw the mouth using a small light line:

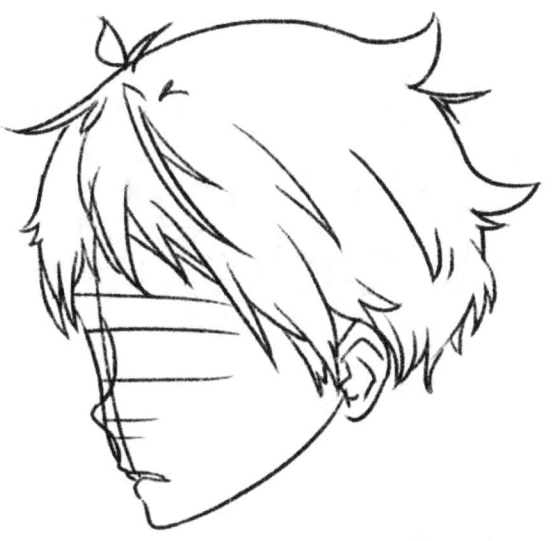

8. Add a small dot to make a nostril:

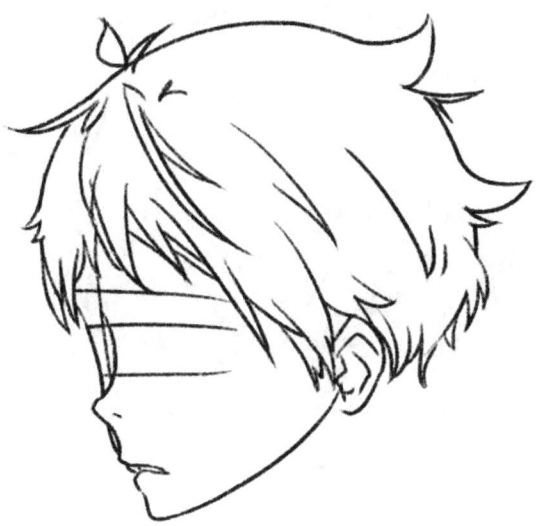

9. Use dark lines to make the eyelashes and eyelids:

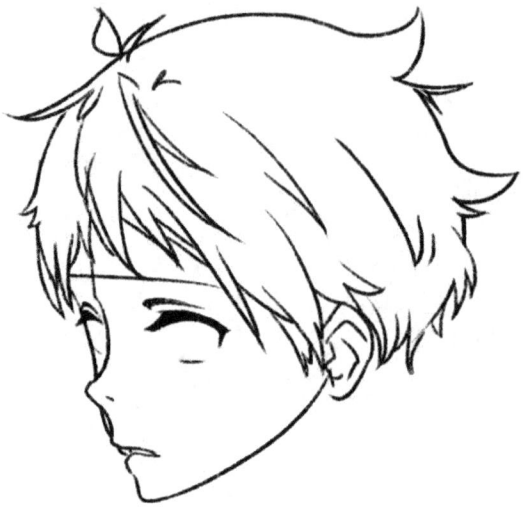

10. Draw and shade circles for the irises leaving small dots for pupils and a highlight:

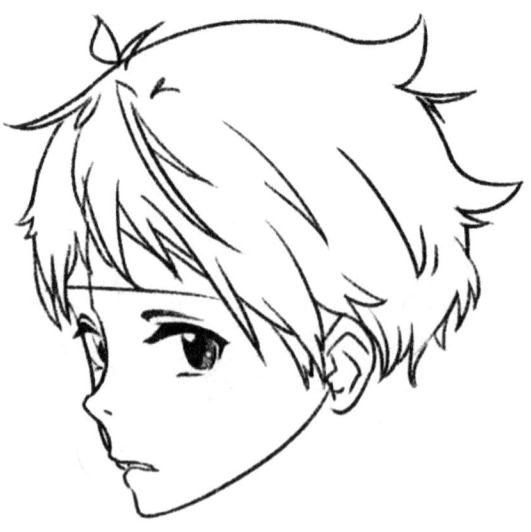

11. Draw a large triangle shape to form the outline of the hood. Draw lines for shoulders:

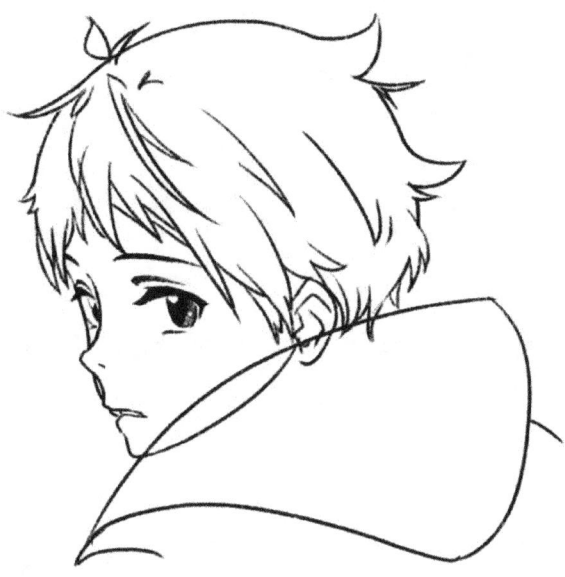

12. Draw more lines to finish detailing the hood:

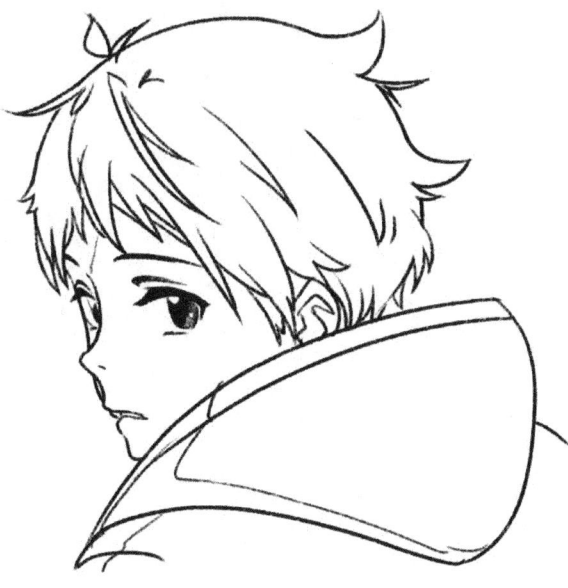

Irritated Girl

1. Start with a small curved line to begin the hair outline:

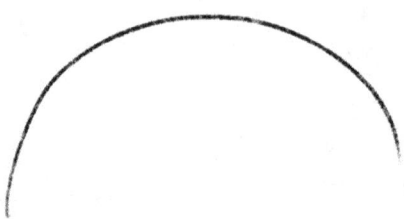

2. Add lines to finish the hair outline. Draw a wide "V" shape for the jaw:

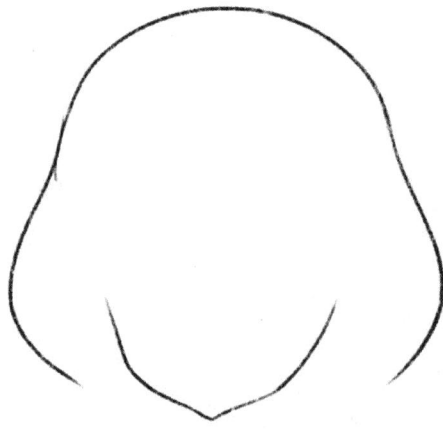

3. Add wavy lines and points to create hair. Draw a line down the center of the face to split it:

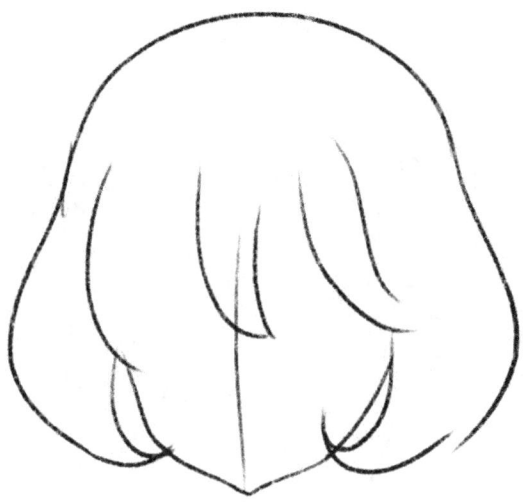

4. Add more lines and points to finish the hair:

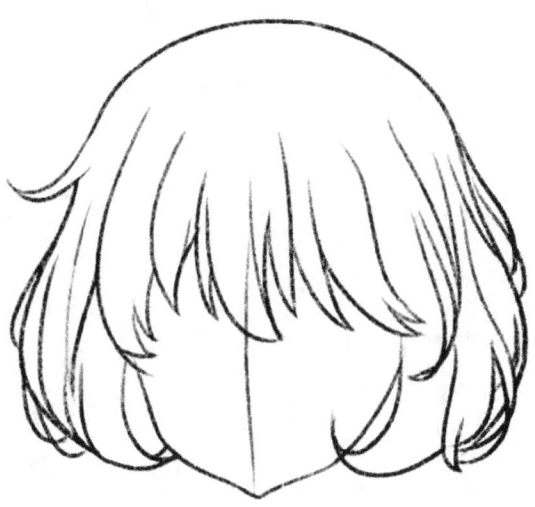

5. Draw arcs to create the shoulders. Use rectangle shapes to form dress straps. Draw lines to make the neck:

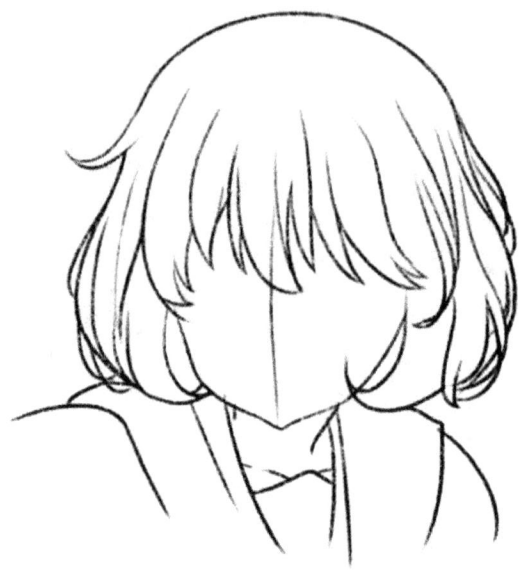

6. Draw guidelines for the eyes and blush marks. Draw the nose:

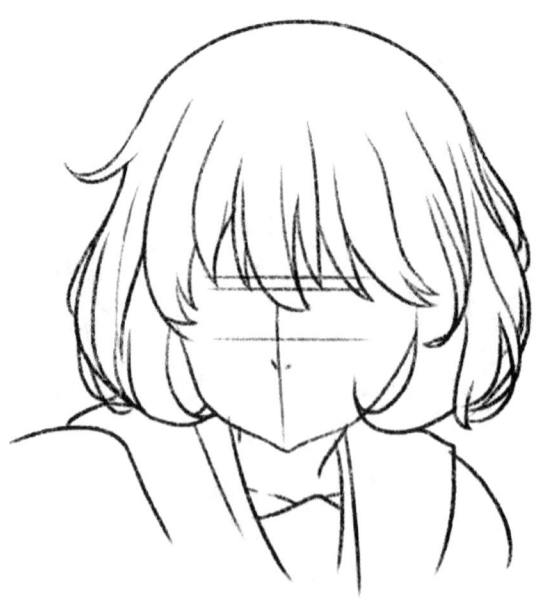

7. Draw thick black lines to make eyelashes. Draw small line to outline the eyes. Draw the mouth:

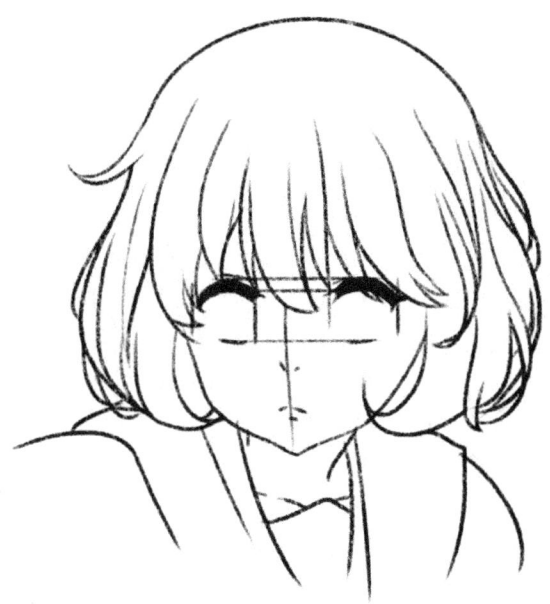

8. Shade in the eyes leaving space for pupils and highlight. Draw thin lines for eyebrows. Draw small lines to create blush marks:

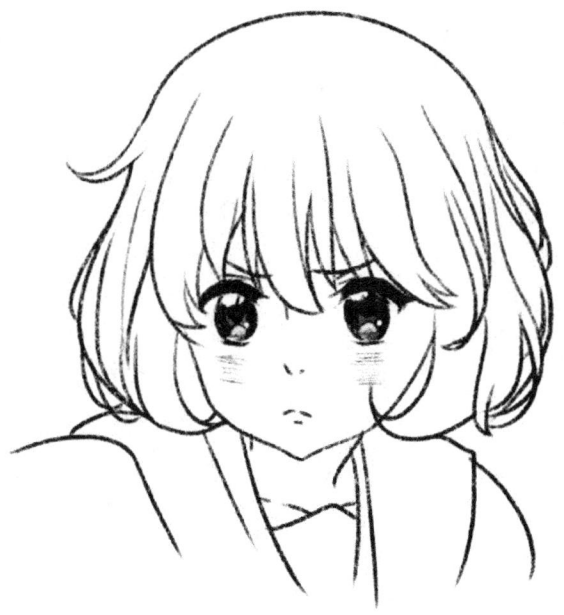

Surprised Boy

1. Outline the head by making a "C" shape:

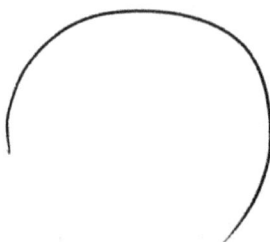

2. Connect lines to the "C" shape to form the face. Draw lines for the neck:

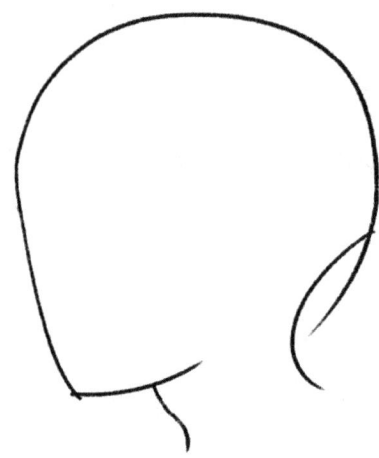

3. Create lines to form shoulders. Use rectangle and triangle shapes to draw the jacket collar and tie:

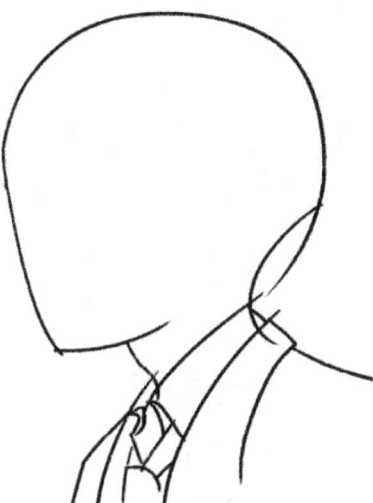

4. Use sharp point to start creating the hair. Draw the ear using oval shapes and hooked lines:

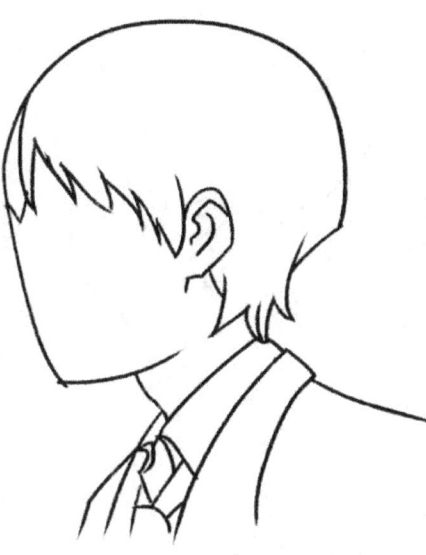

5. Add spiky lines to detail the hair:

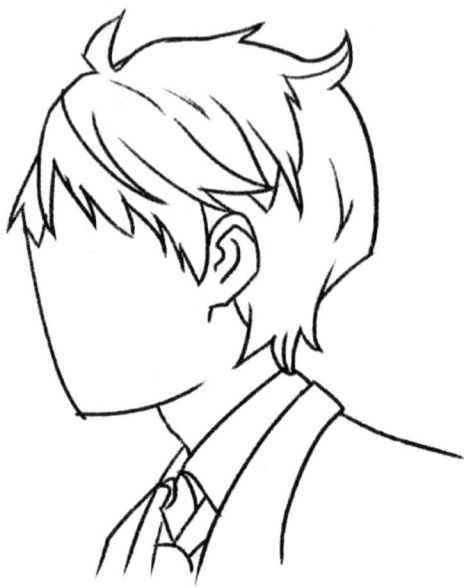

6. Contour the face inward to create the nose. Draw a "U" shape for the mouth:

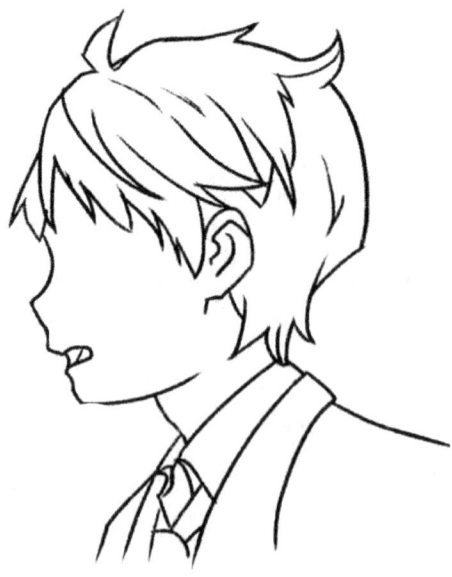

7. Draw thick lines with a small line to outline the eyes:

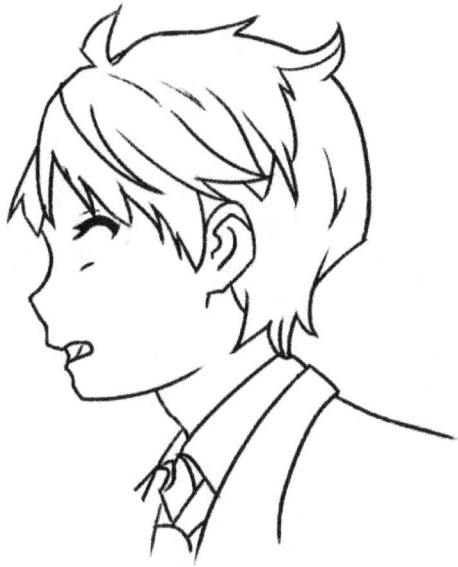

8. Create a dark oval shape for the eye. Shade in the mouth. Draw the eyebrows:

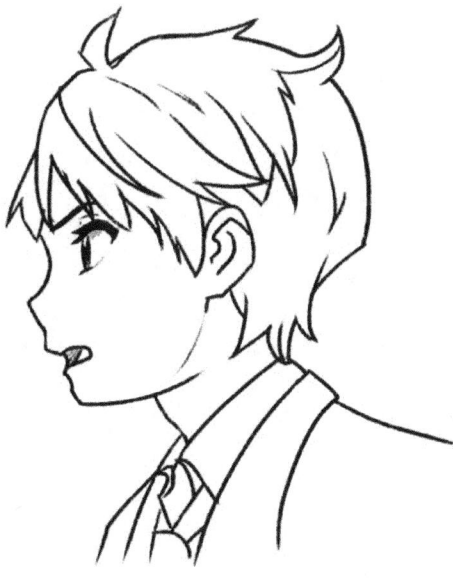

9. Finish detailing the hair and add lines to contour the shoulder:

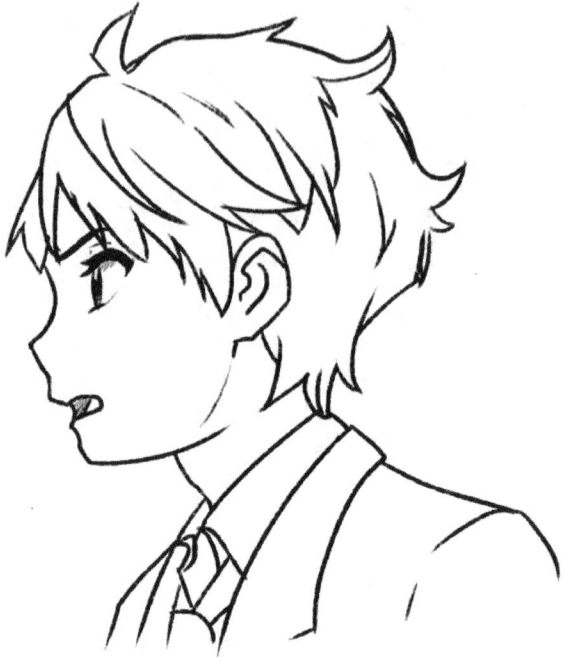

Irate Boy

1. Draw a "C" shape to form the hair outline:

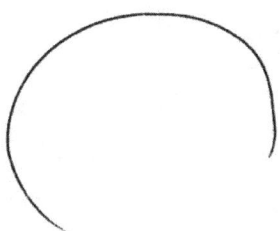

2. Draw lines to make the face leaving space the ear. Draw a line down the face's center:

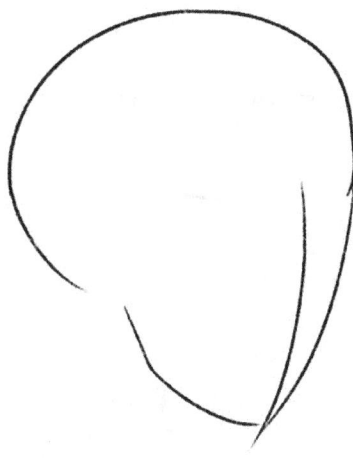

3. Use sharp lines to outline the hair. Draw the ear using an oval shape and thin lines:

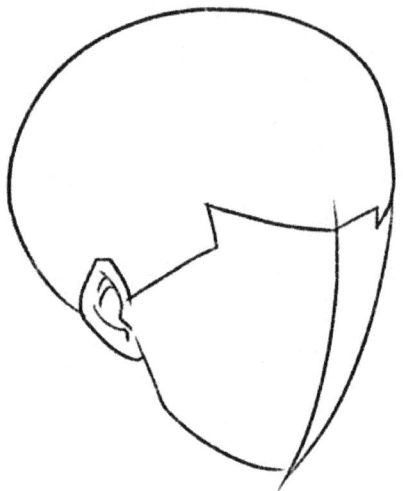

4. Draw guidelines for the facial features:

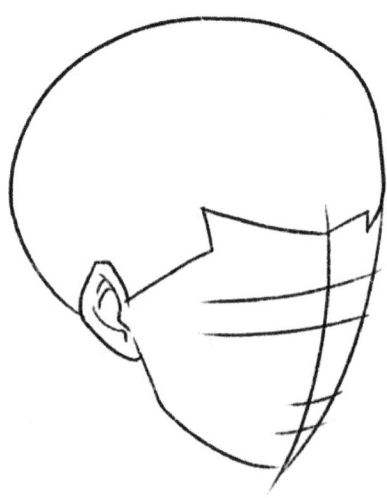

5. Draw steep slanted lines for the eyebrows. Draw a "V" shape for the nose:

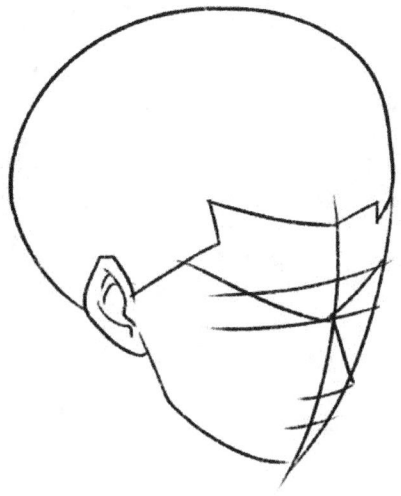

6. Draw sharp lines to create hair:

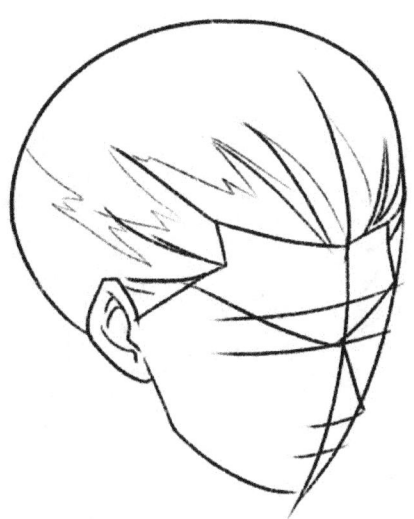

7. Add more sharp lines and points to give the hair more detail:

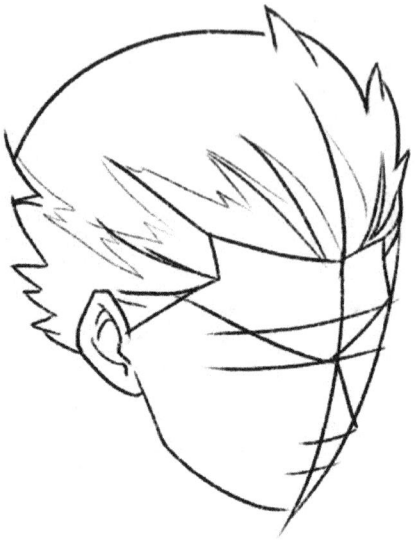

8. Add more detail to the hair. Draw lines for the mouth:

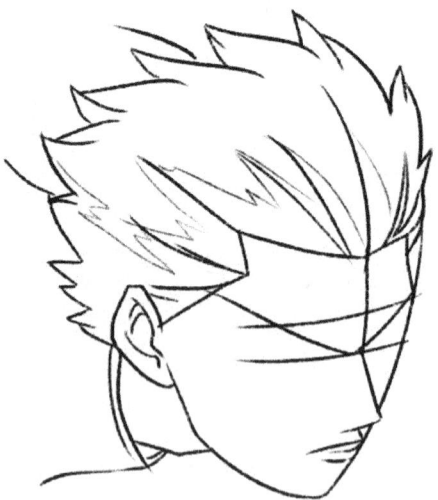

9. Draw almond shapes to outline the eyes. Draw lines for the eyebrows:

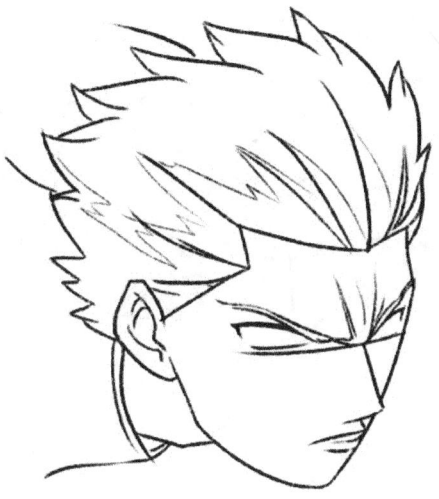

10. Add circles for the eyes:

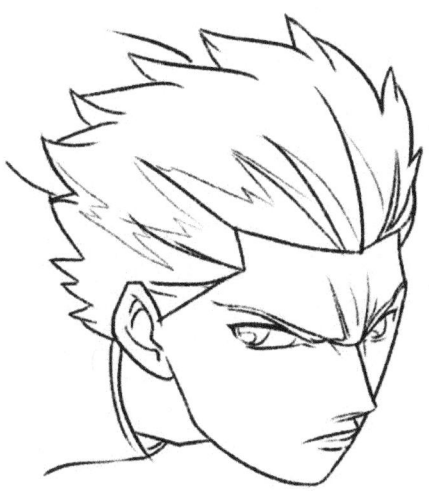

11. Shade in eyes leaving space for pupils:

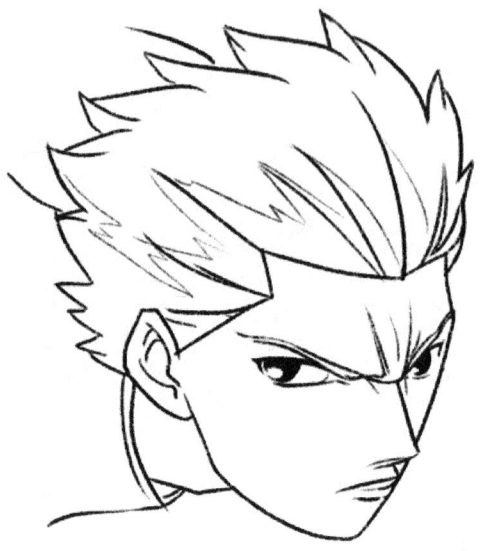

Shouting Boy

1. Draw a "C" shape to begin the outline of the hair:

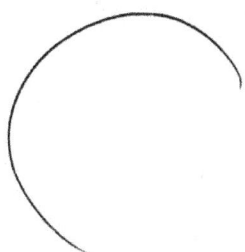

2. Complete the hair outline. Add lines in a "V" shape for the face:

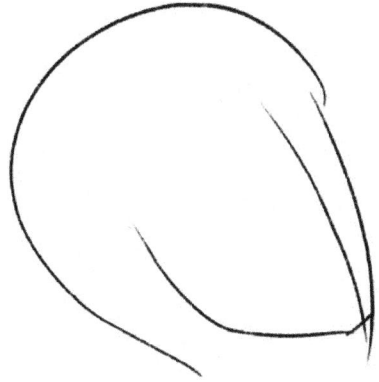

3. Using sharp lines and arcs draw the ear. Draw lines to make the neck:

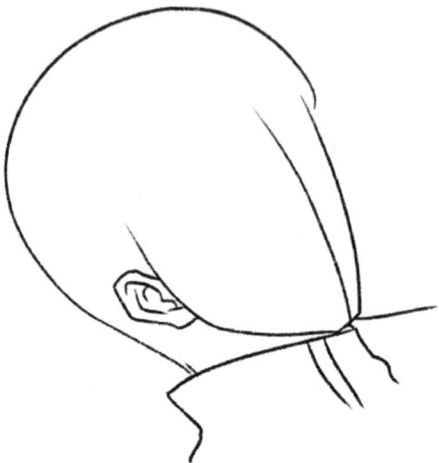

4. Draw guidelines for the facial features:

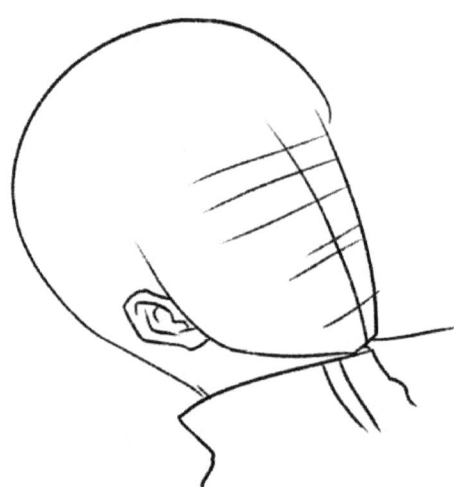

5. Draw jagged, sharp lines to begin shaping the hair:

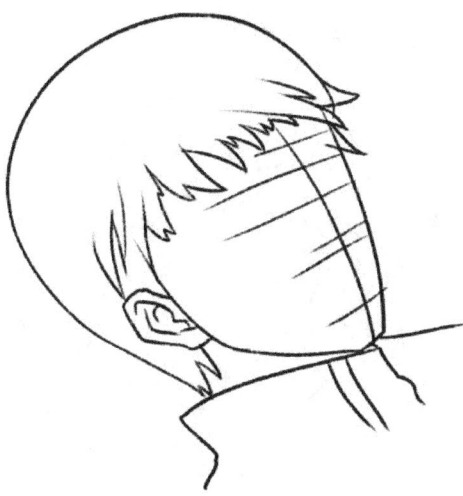

6. Add slight arcs to contour the face:

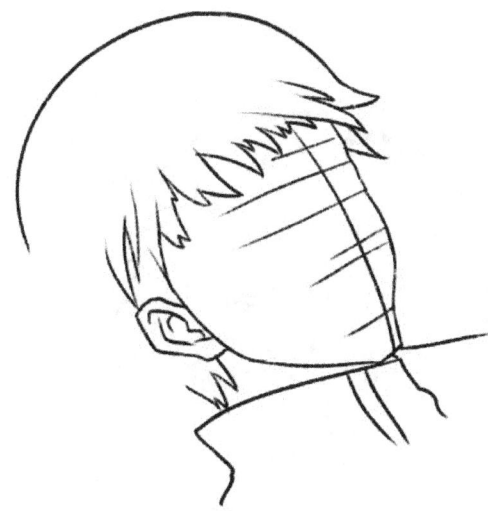

7. Finish detailing the hair by adding more sharp lines:

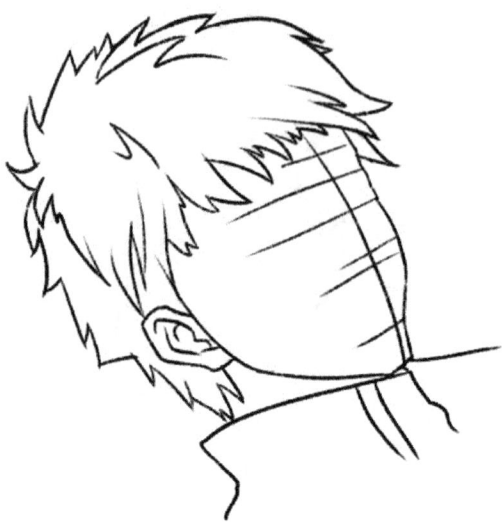

8. Draw semi-circle shapes with lines underneath to outline the eyes:

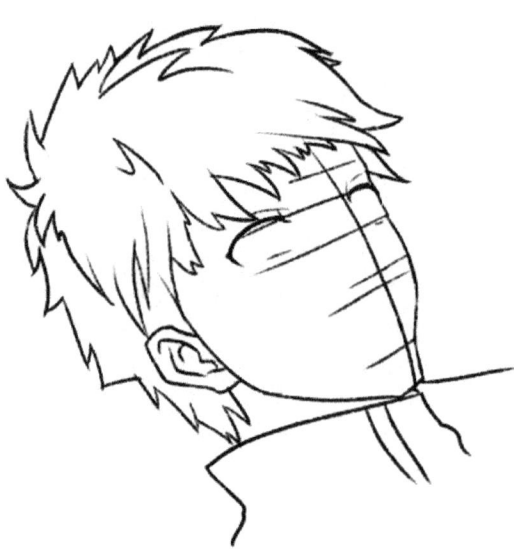

9. Erase the guideline between the eyes:

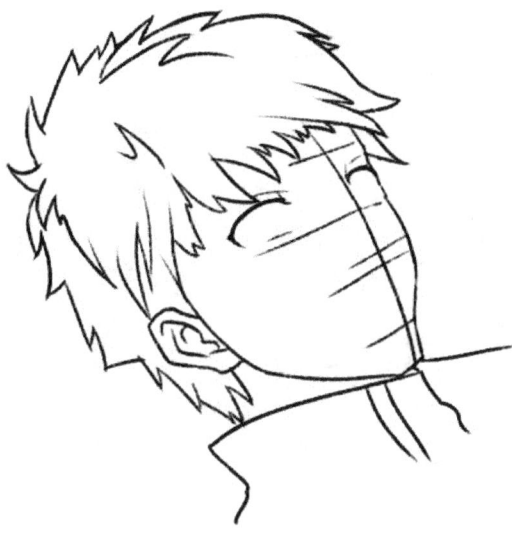

10. Add circles to form the eyes. Draw thick dark lines to make eyebrows:

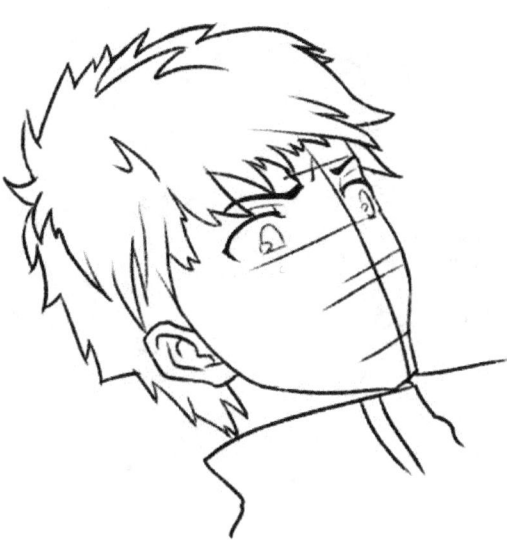

11. Draw a small wide "V" shape to form the nose:

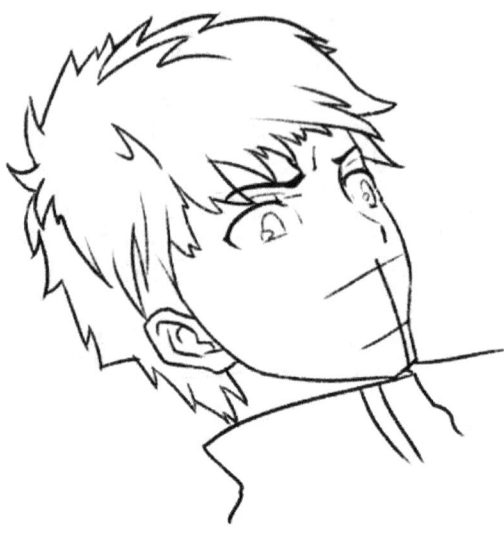

12. Using the lower two guidelines, form connecting lines to create the mouth:

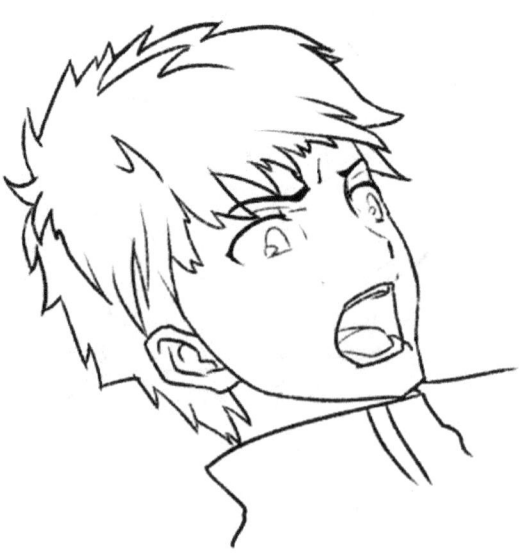

13. Shade in the eyes leaving space for the pupil:

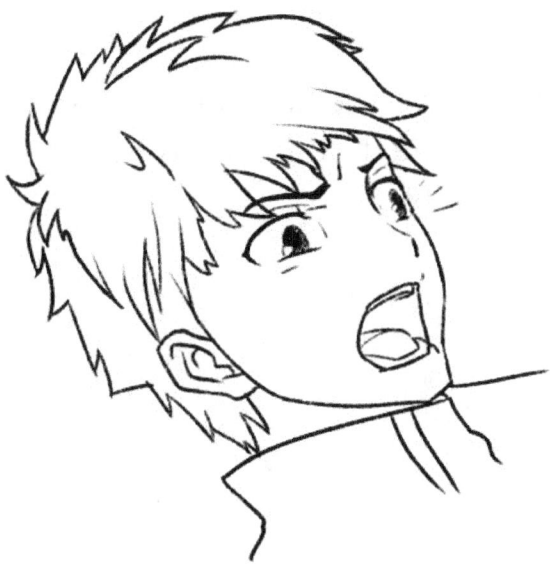

Part 3: Sitting Guys

Sullen Girl

1. Draw "C" like shape for the hair outline. Draw lines to form the jaw. Make a "T" in the middle of the face for facial feature guidelines:

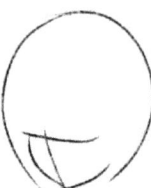

2. Draw lines to create the shoulders. Draw lines in an hour glass shape for the torso:

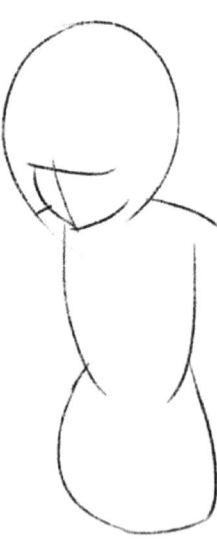

3. Draw rectangle lines to form the arms and small square shapes to form the hands:

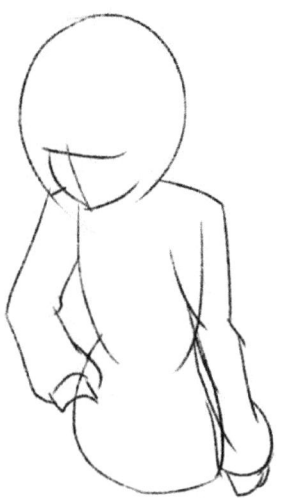

4. Draw long lines to make legs. Draw an oval shape for the foot:

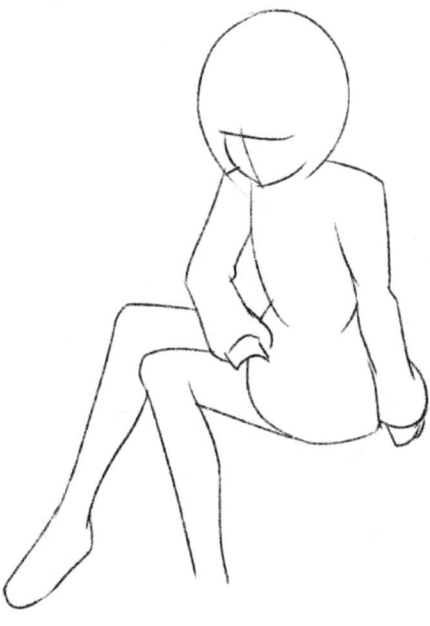

5. Draw an oval shape for the other foot. Draw lines to make fingers:

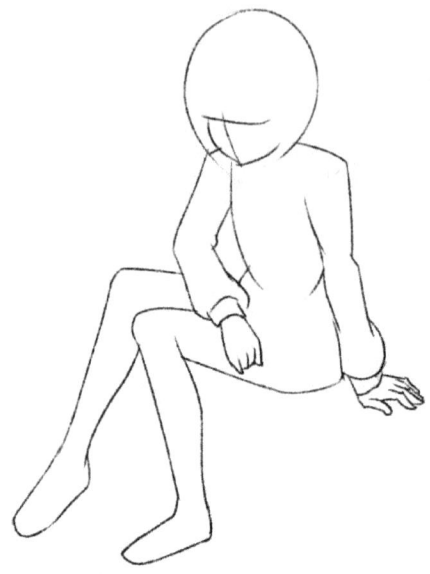

6. Draw wrinkle lines and triangle shapes to form the shirt collar:

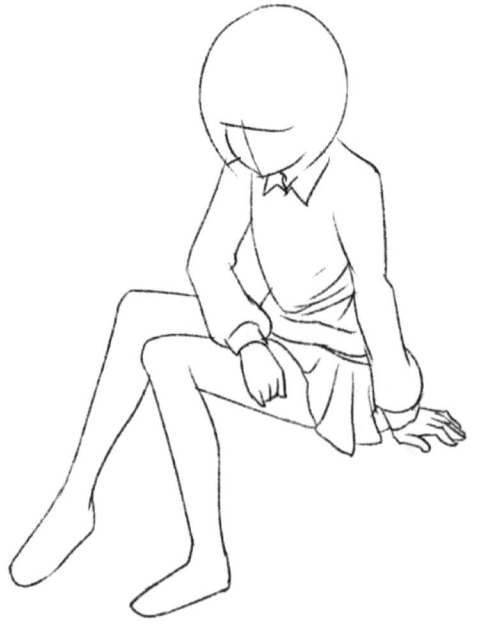

7. Draw more wrinkle lines and add small lines for knees on the legs:

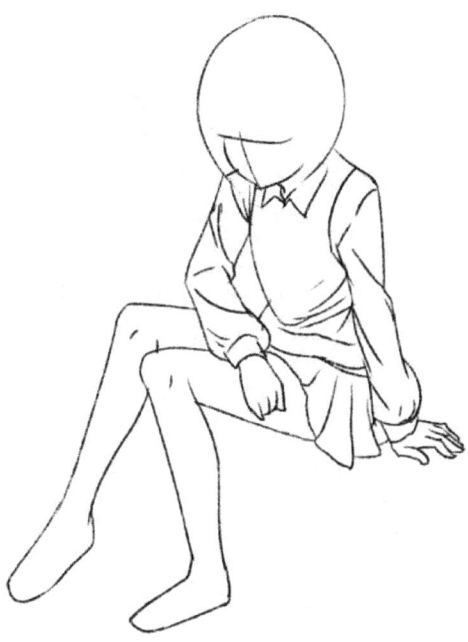

8. Draw jagged lines with points to make hair:

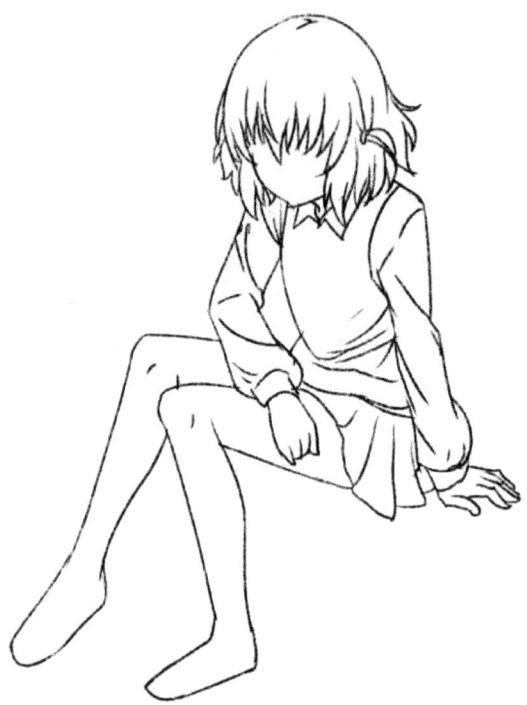

9. Draw lines to make the eyes, nose, and mouth:

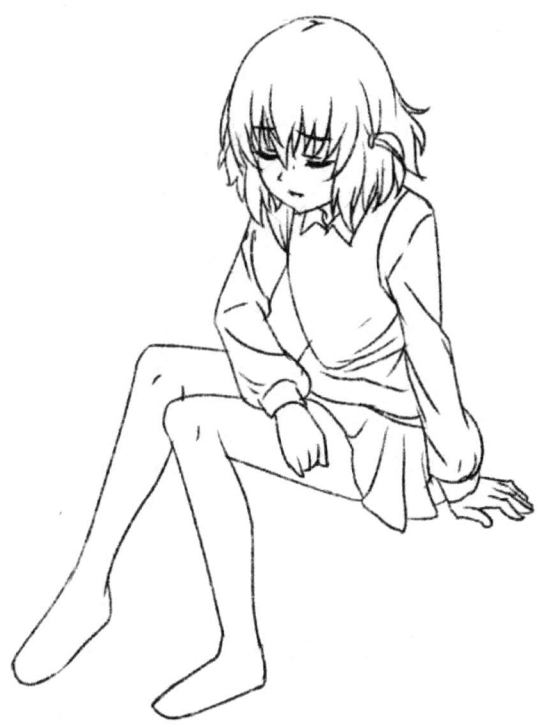

10. Finish detailing the clothes and add shoes on the feet:

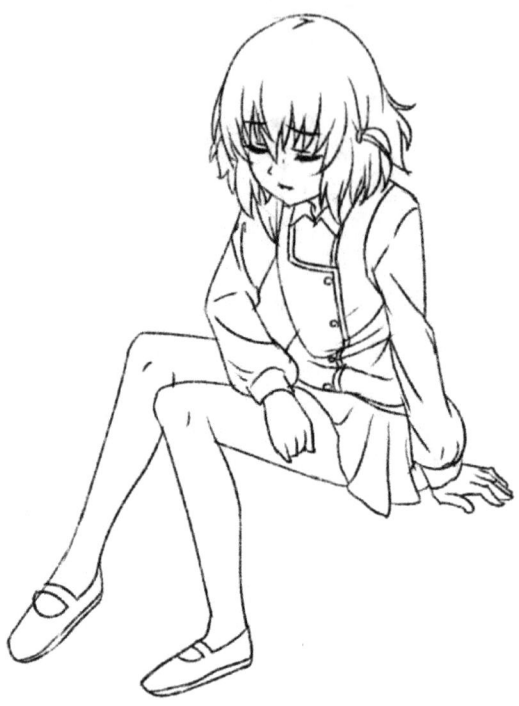

Studious Girl

1. Draw a hook like shape to form the head and spine:

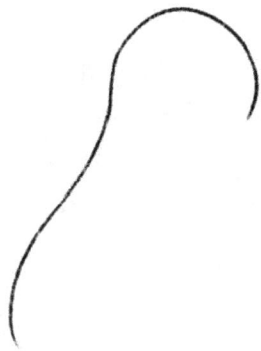

2. Add curves and sharp angles to contour the face:

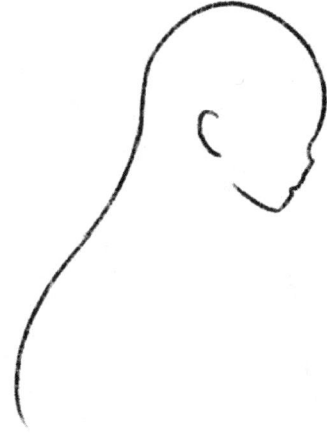

3. Draw a series of long and short lines to make hair:

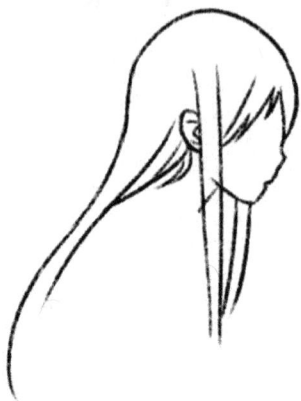

4. Draw lines to outline the torso and chest:

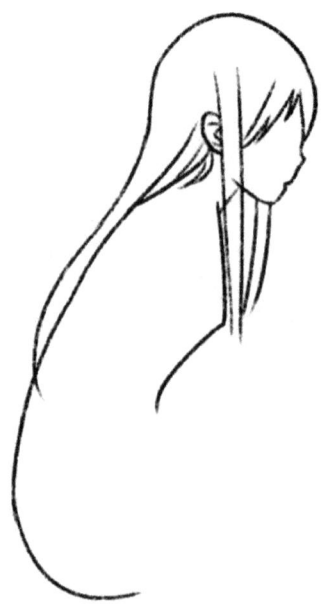

5. Add lines to outline the waist:

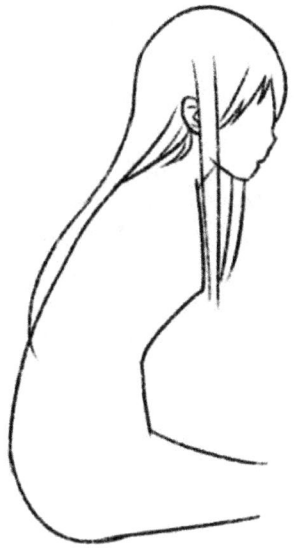

6. Draw thin rectangle shaped lines to make legs:

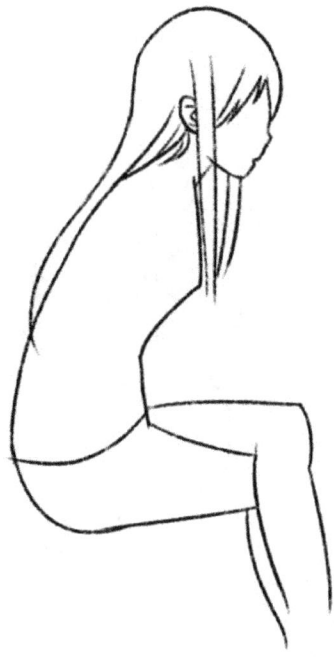

7. Draw "V" like shapes to form an arm and then draw the hand:

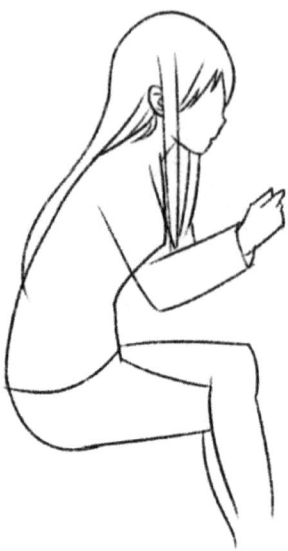

8. Use dark lines to form the eyes and eyebrows. Draw a rectangle shape to make the book:

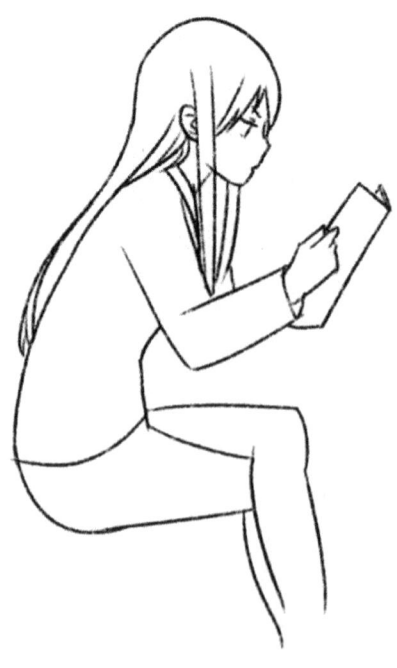

9. Add wrinkle lines and small arcs to make buttons:

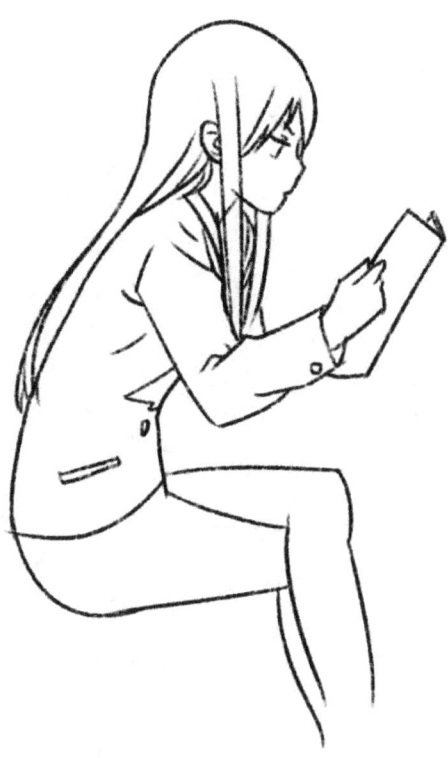

10. Draw a triangle shape to create the skirt. Draw socks on the legs:

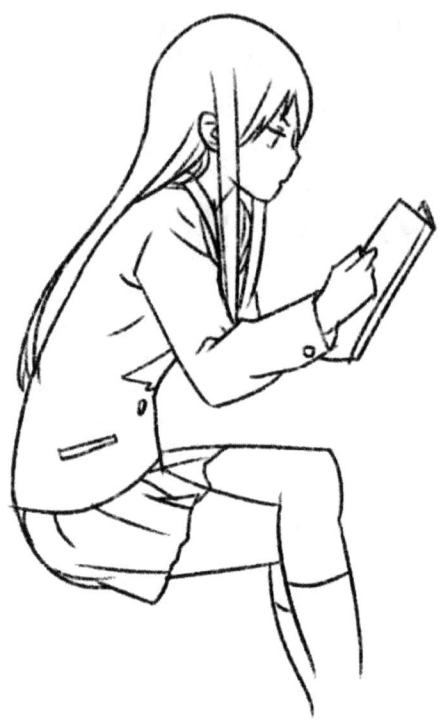

11. Using rectangle and square shapes make shoes. Draw vertical lines to outline the desk:

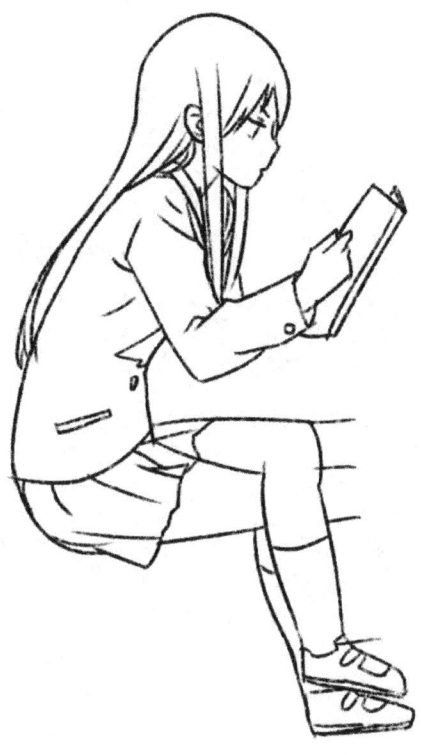

12. Finish the desk by adding more lines. Draw thin rectangle shapes to make the chair:

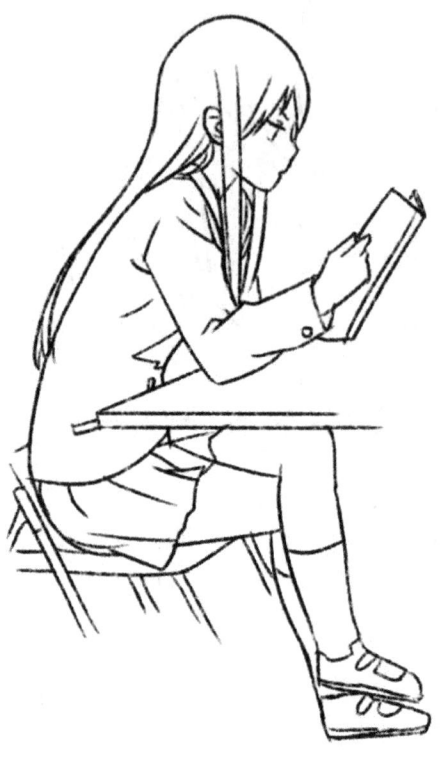

Bored Boy

1. Draw a shape that resembles an upside-down tear drop to make the head:

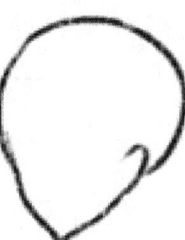

2. Draw a wide rectangle to outline the upper body:

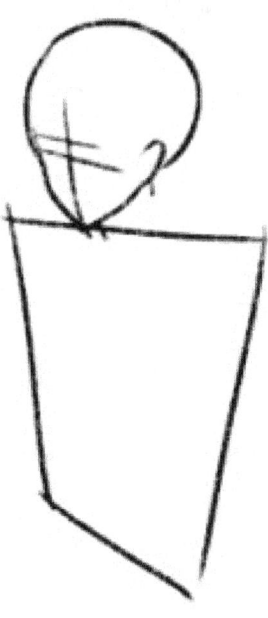

3. Draw lines with a "V" in between them to create thighs:

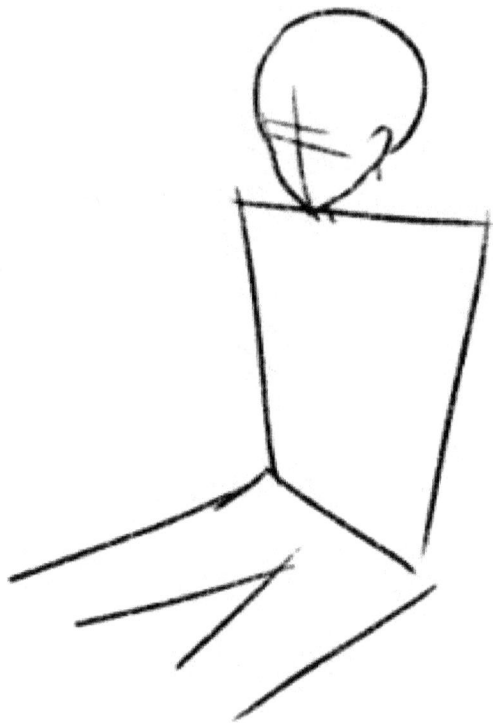

4. Draw lines to make the arms and hands:

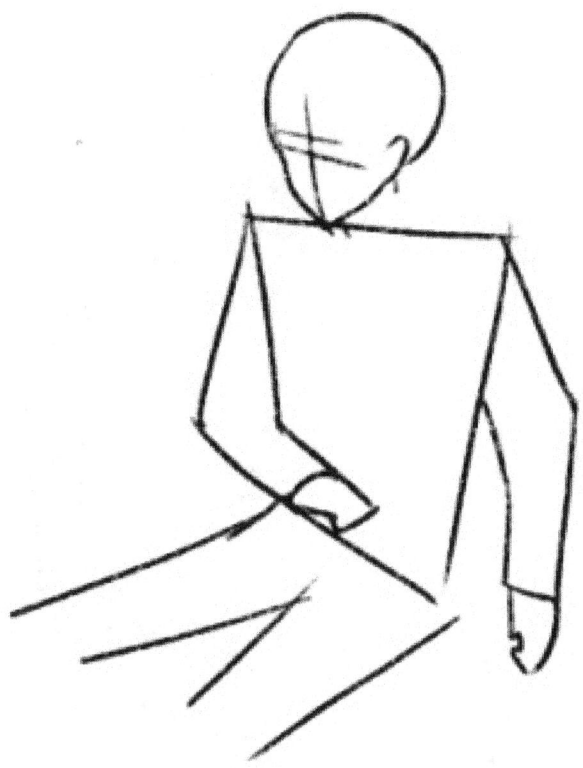

5. Draw rectangle shapes for the legs and feet. Draw lines to create the shoulders:

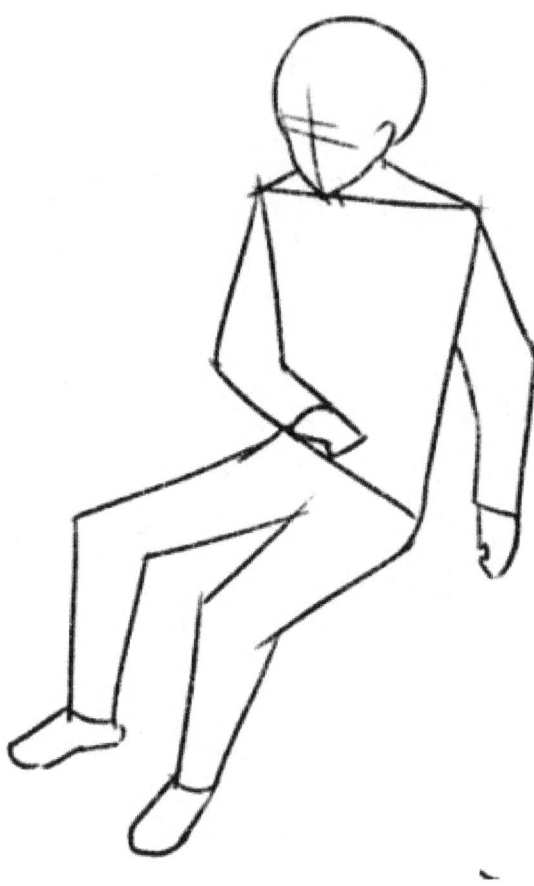

6. Draw lines to form the jacket. Use triangle shapes to make the collar:

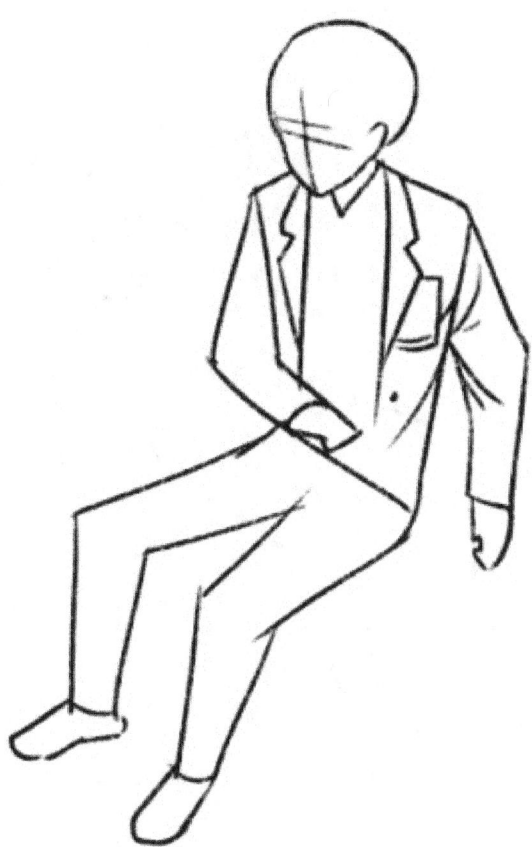

7. Add "V" shapes to make the vest. Draw more triangle shapes for the shirt collar:

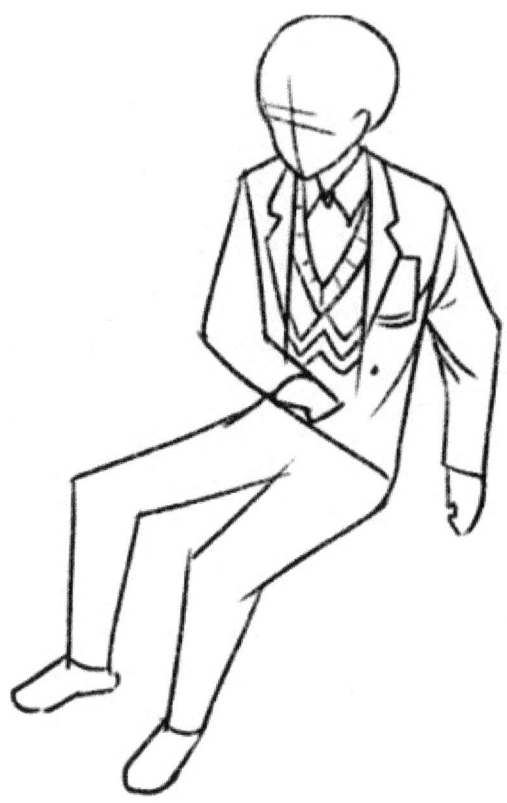

8. Create wrinkle lines on the pants. Draw lines to make shoes:

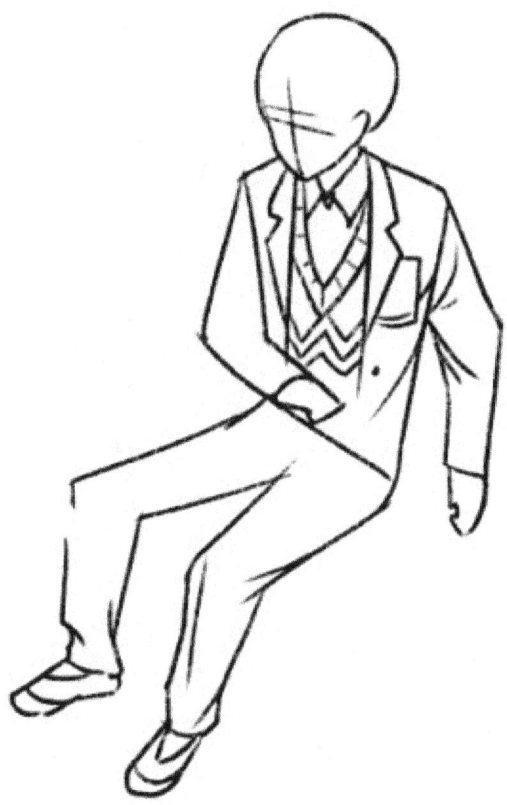

9. Use small lines to make fingers:

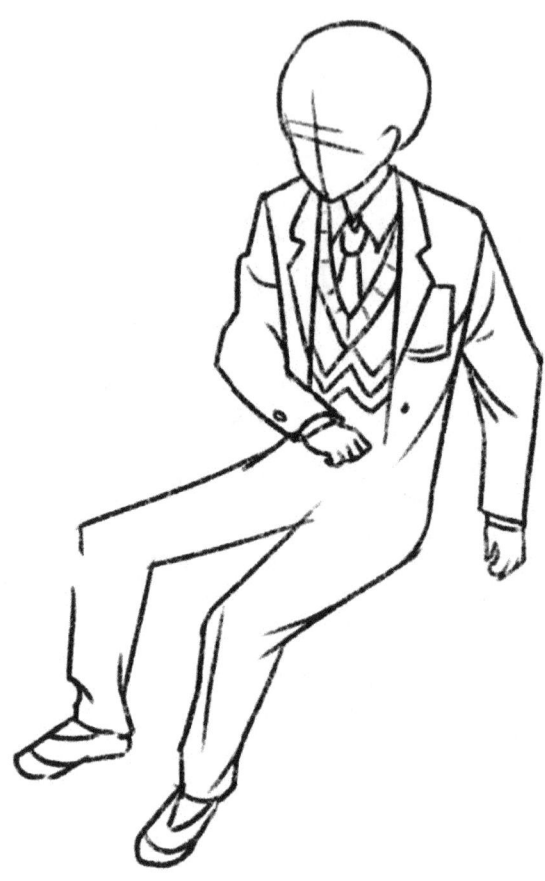

10. Draw jagged lines and points to make hair:

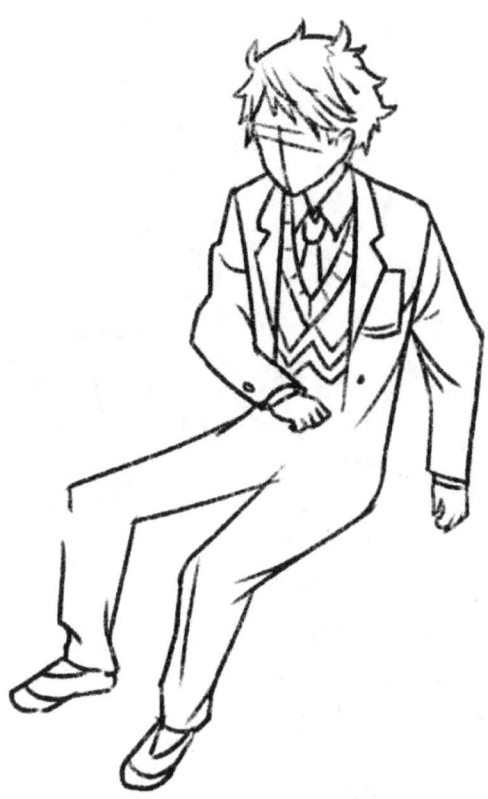

11. Draw small dots, lines, and circles to create facial features:

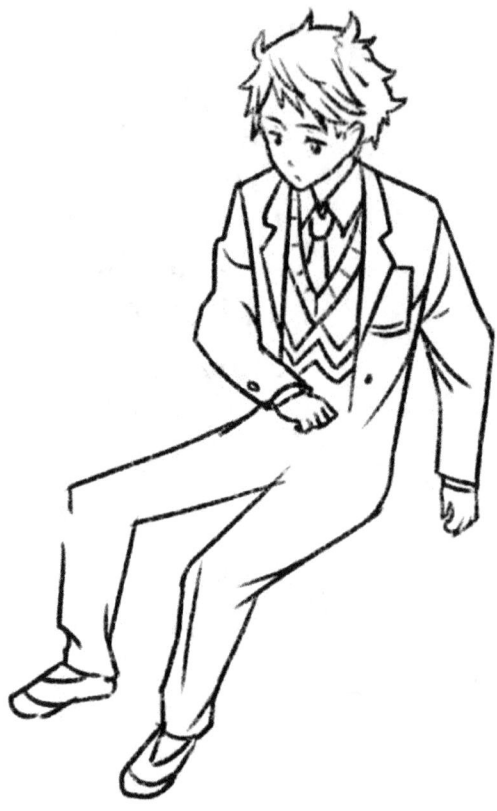

12. Draw a rectangle shape to create the desk:

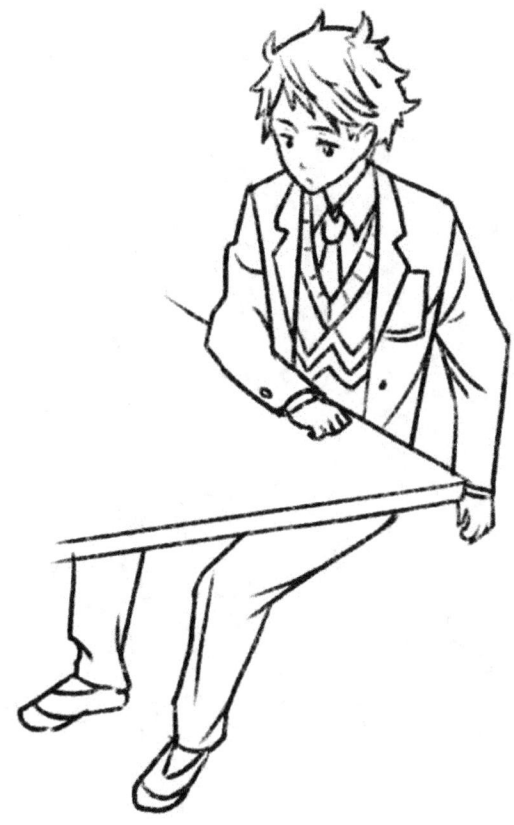

13. Draw thin lines and a rectangle shape to make a chair:

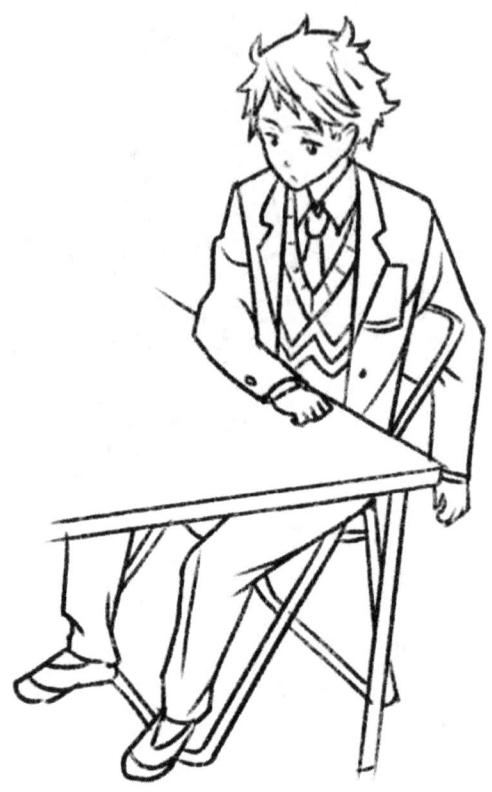

Part 4: Moving Poses

Screaming Boy

1. Draw an upside down tear shape to form the head. Draw a slanted line to outline the shoulders:

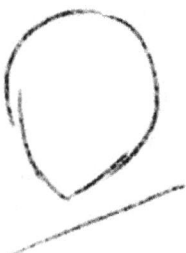

2. Draw a "V" like shape to create the right arm:

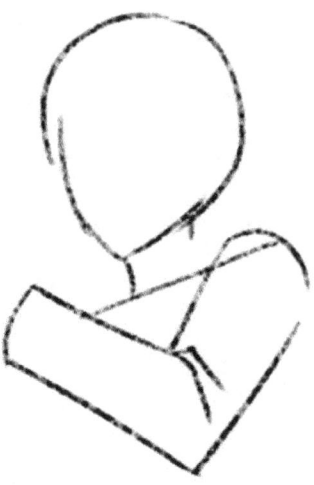

3. Draw a long "U" shape to create an outline for the torso and right leg:

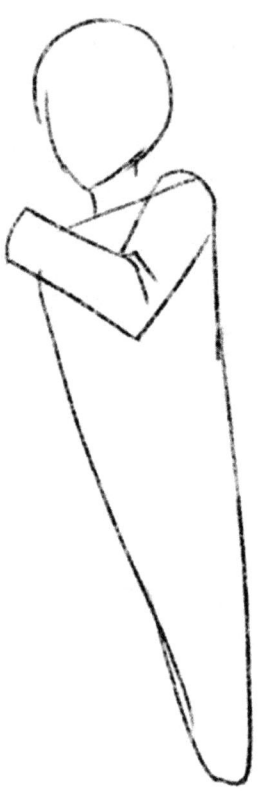

4. Add lines to form the left leg. Draw a dark vertical line to separate the legs and torso:

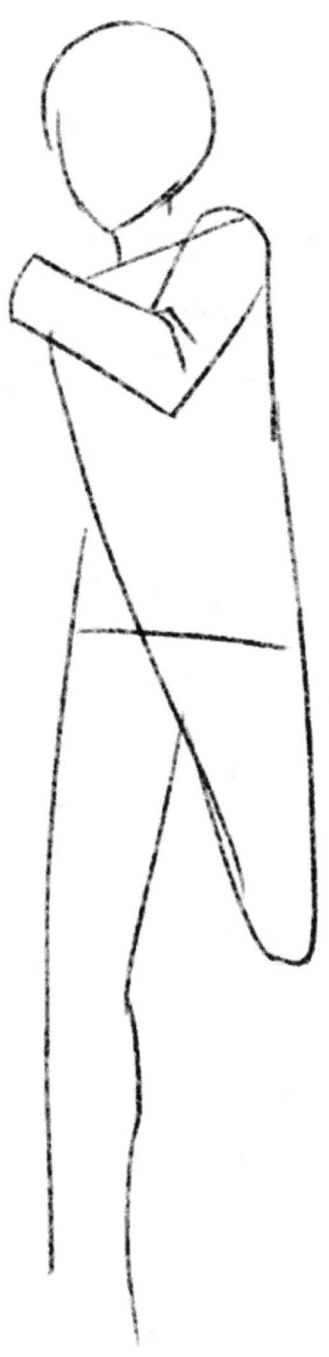

5. Draw the second arm. Add hands and fingers:

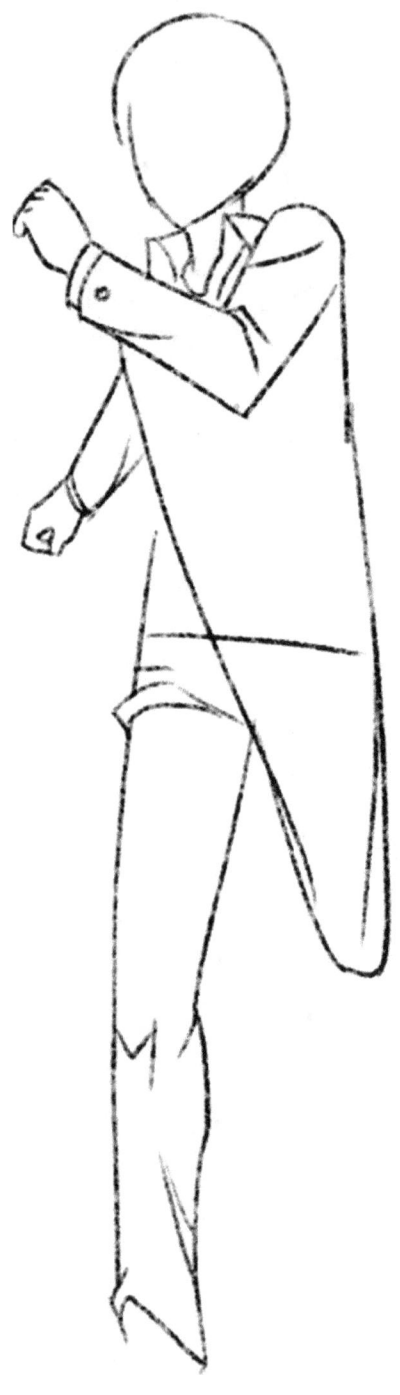

6. Draw jagged lines to form hair. Draw triangle shapes to make a collar. Add facial features:

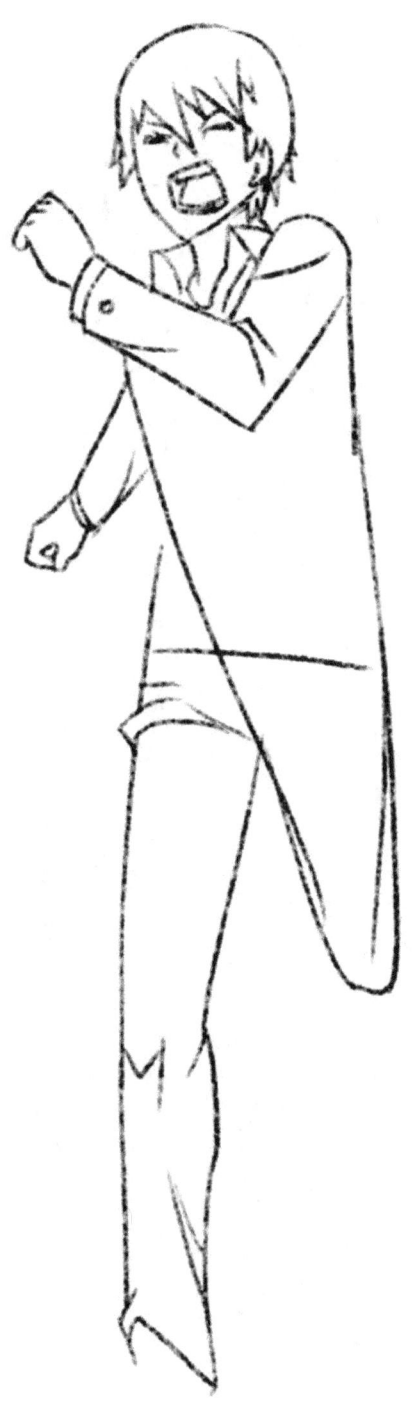

7. Draw oval shapes for feet. Draw curved lines for the jacket:

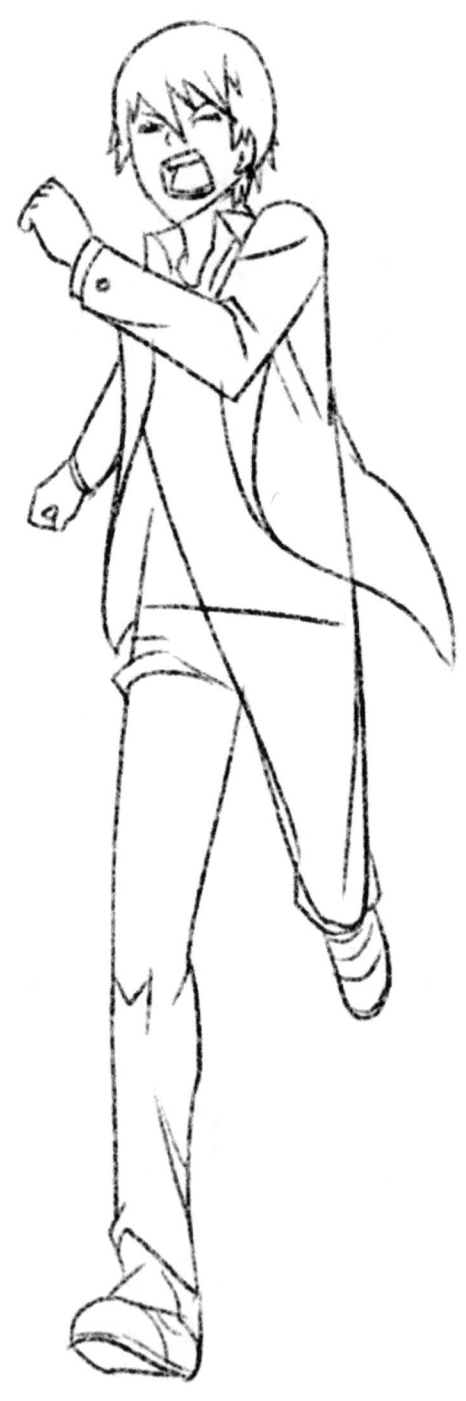

8. Erase dark torso line. Add more detail to clothing:

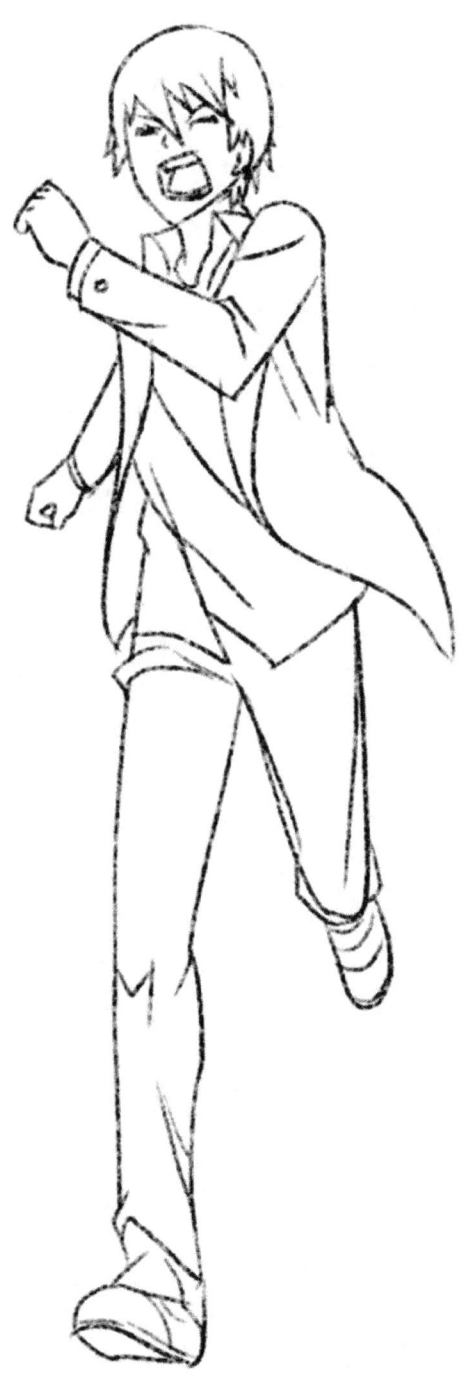

9. Add a bit more detail to the clothing:

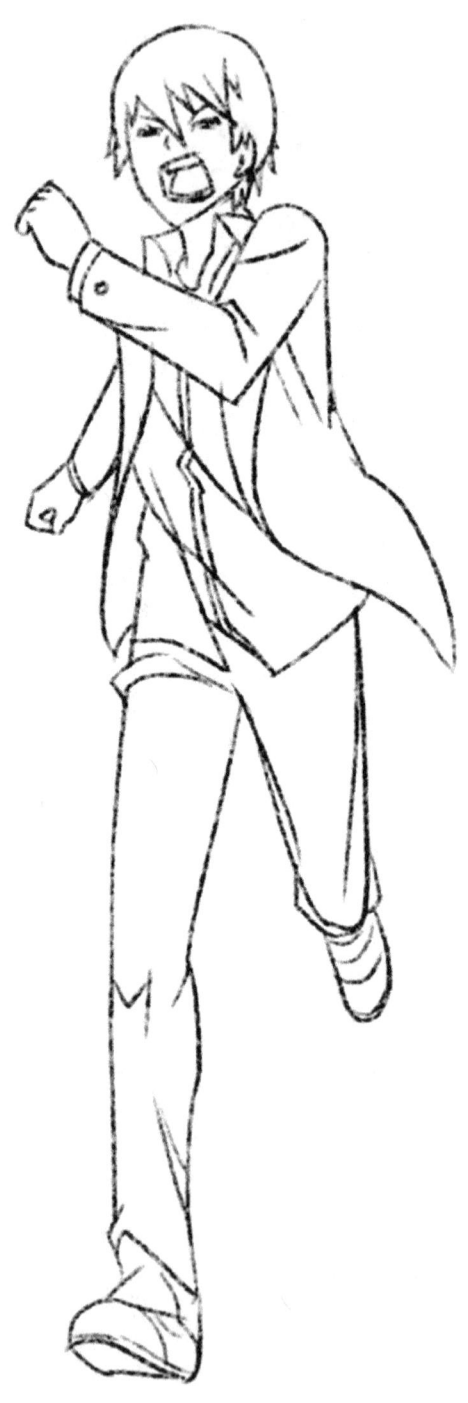

Infuriated Boy

1. Draw upside tear drop to form the head. Add a "T" for feature guidelines:

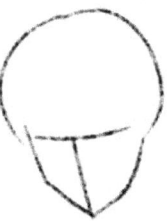

2. Draw a rectangle shape with arcs at the top to make the torso:

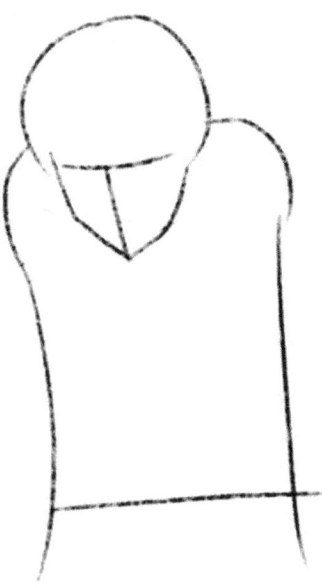

3. Draw rectangle shapes for the thighs:

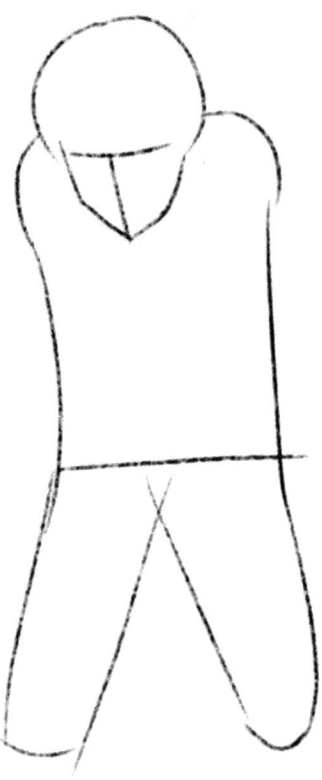

4. Draw cylinder shapes for the arms:

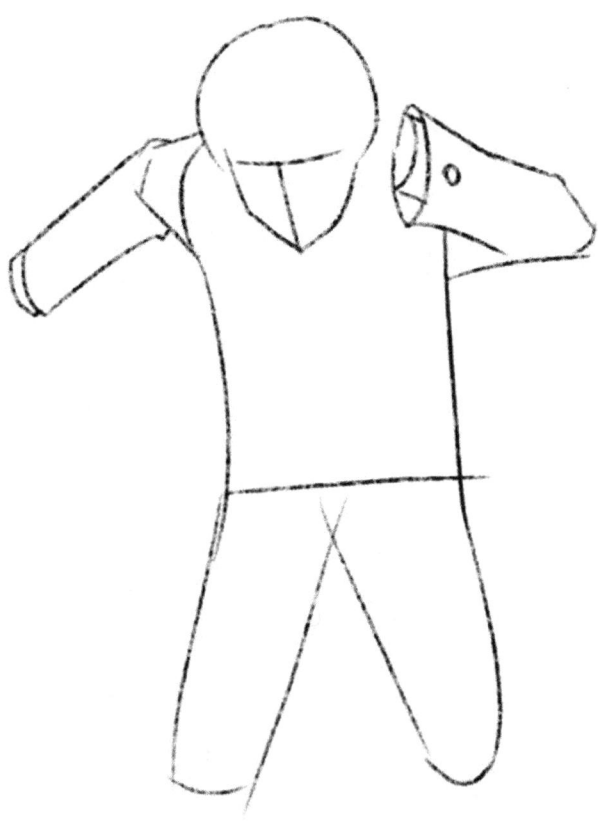

5. Use oval shapes to draw a foot and use oval shapes for the hands:

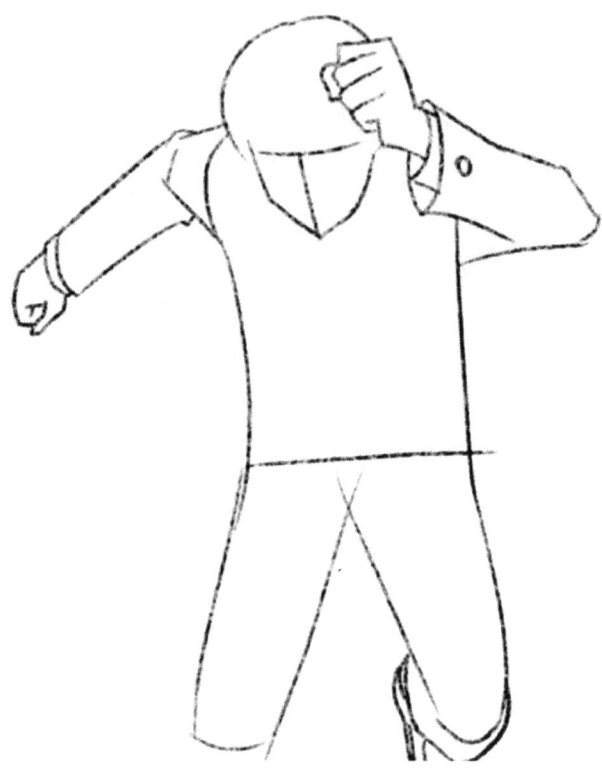

6. Use lines to make the left leg. Detail the clothes:

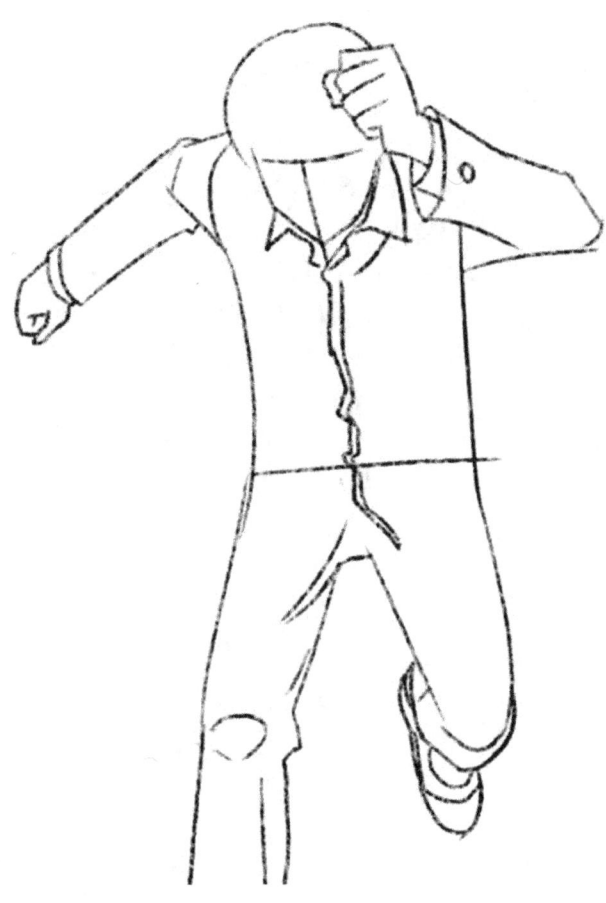

7. Use sharp points to create hair. Add more detail to the clothing:

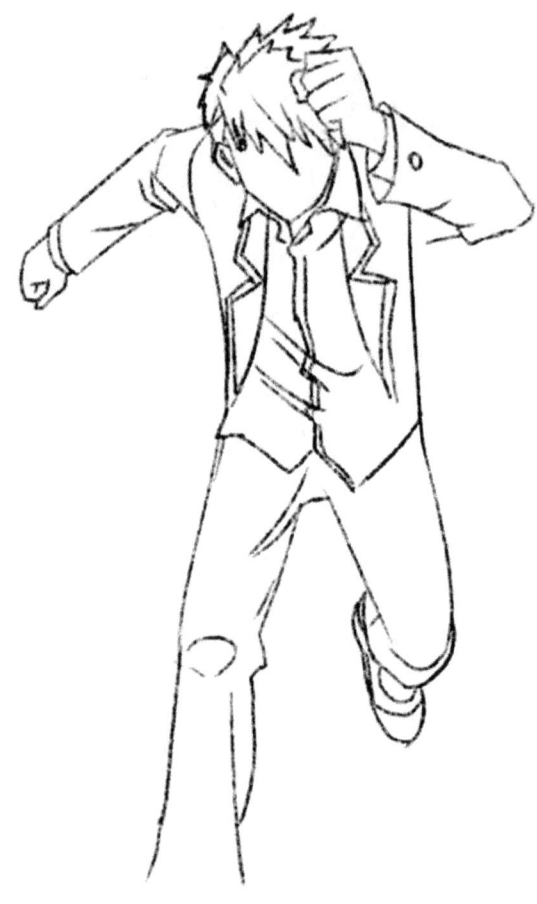

8. Add more lines to finish the jacket:

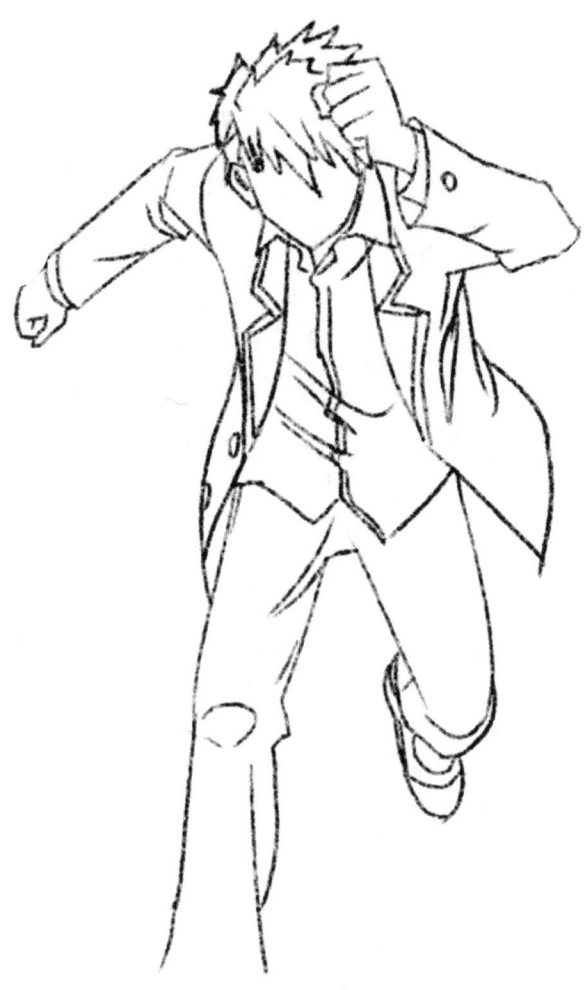

9. Draw facial feature using triangles, circles and lines:

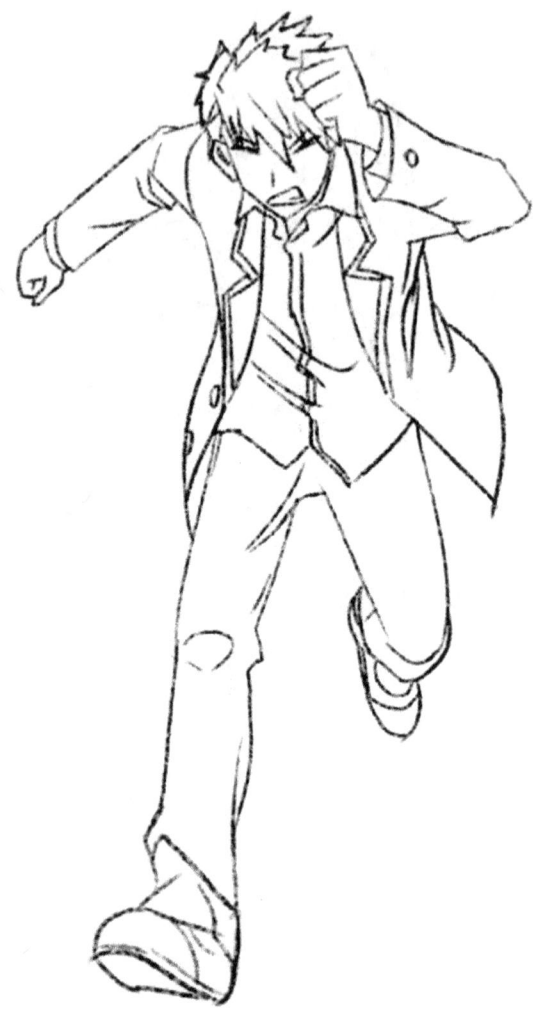

Curious Girl

1. Draw lines to outline the hair and face:

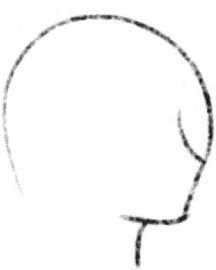

2. Use swerving lines to make hair. Draw slanted lines to outline the torso:

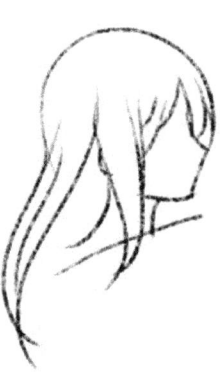

3. Draw lines to outline the arms:

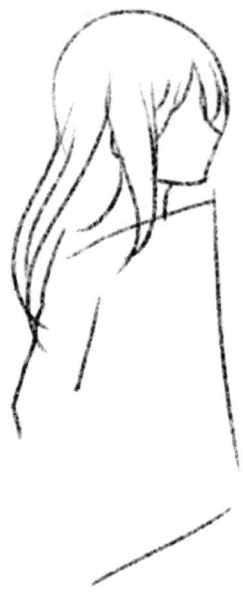

4. Draw rectangle shapes to make the left arm. Contour the torso:

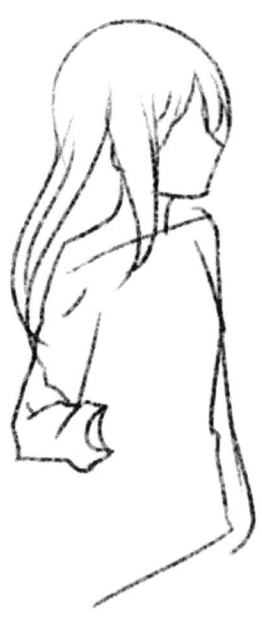

5. Draw lines to outline the legs:

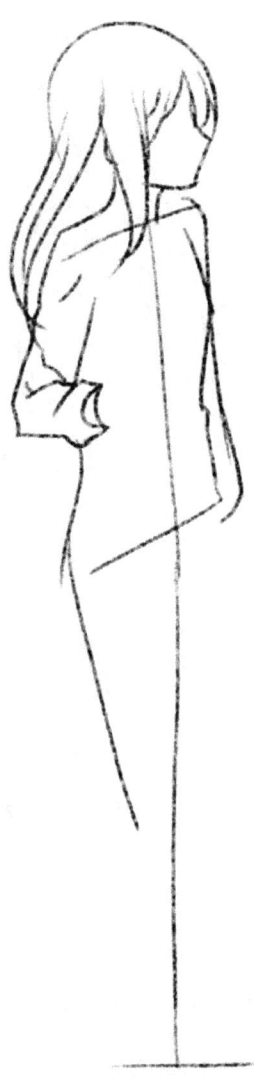

6. Draw a triangle shape for the skirt and contour the legs:

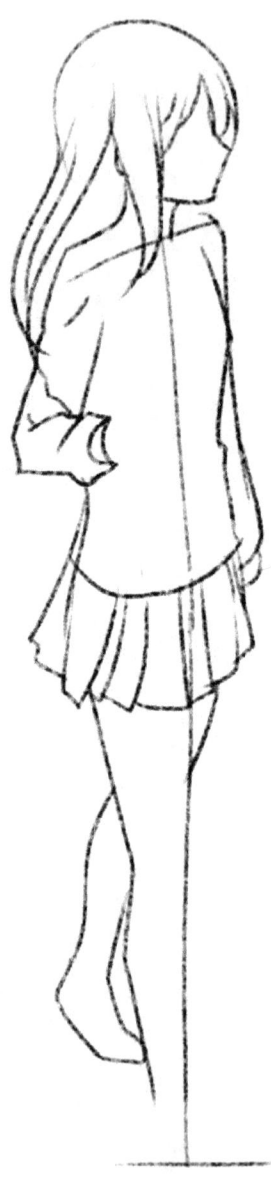

7. Draw lines to make the bag handle:

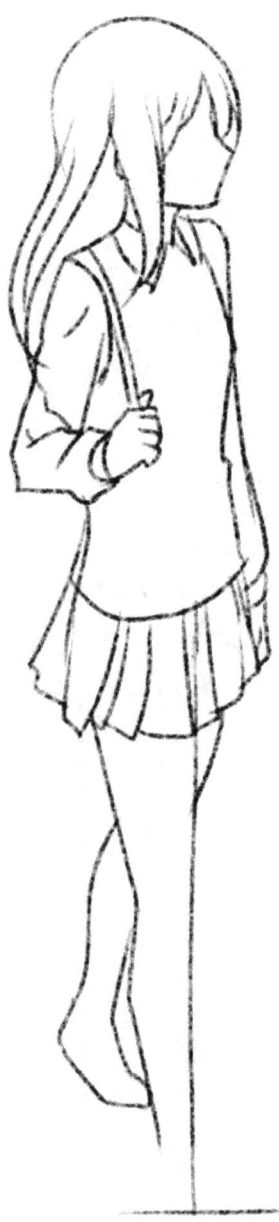

8. Draw a rectangle shape to make the bag:

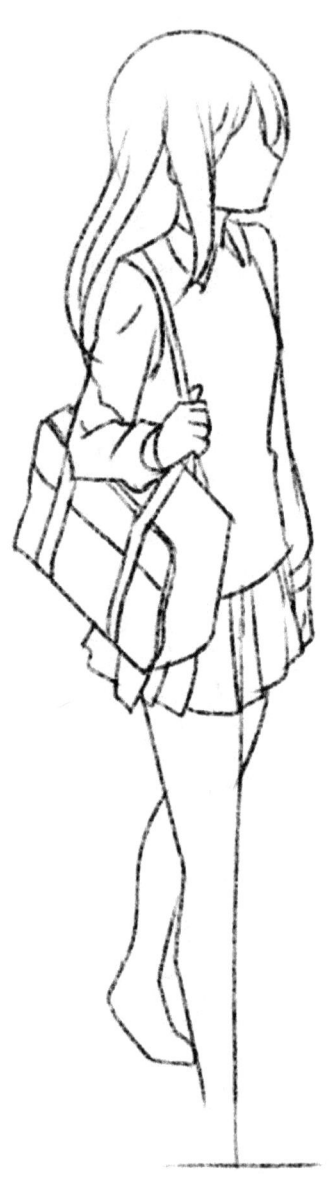

9. Detail bag. Add lines to make socks:

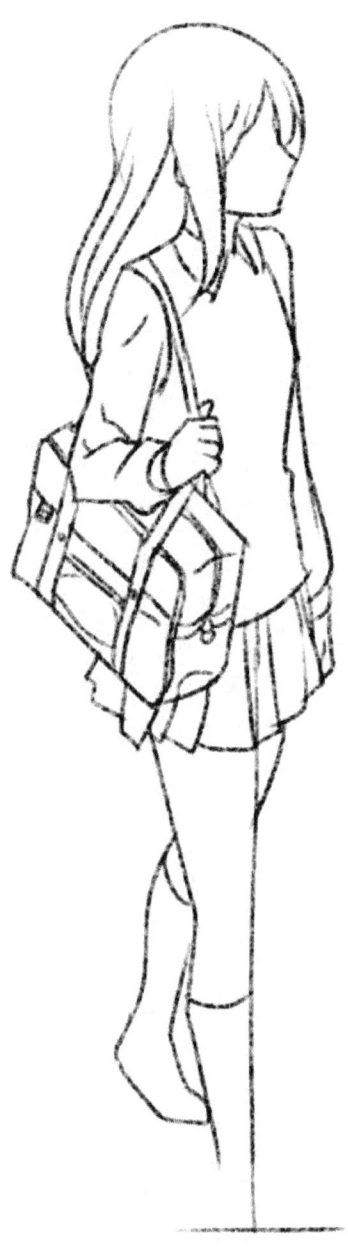

10. Use oval shapes to draw shoes:

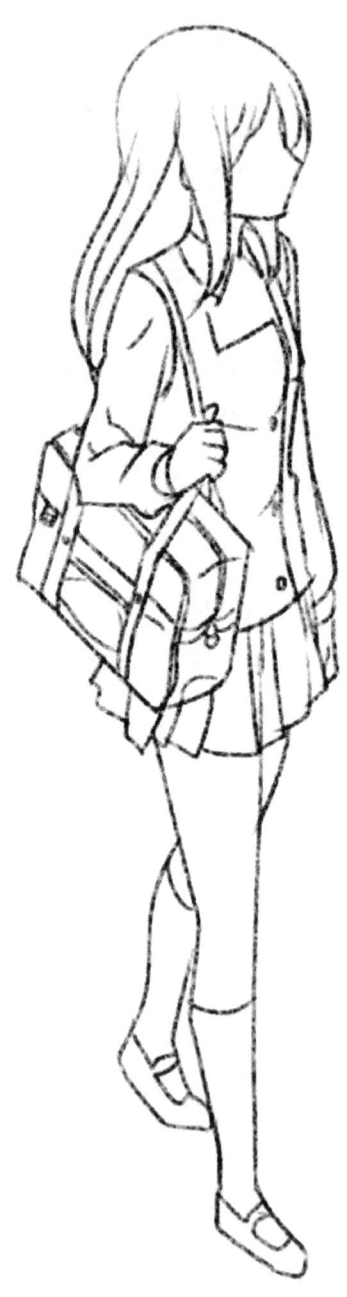

11. Draw eyes, nose and mouth:

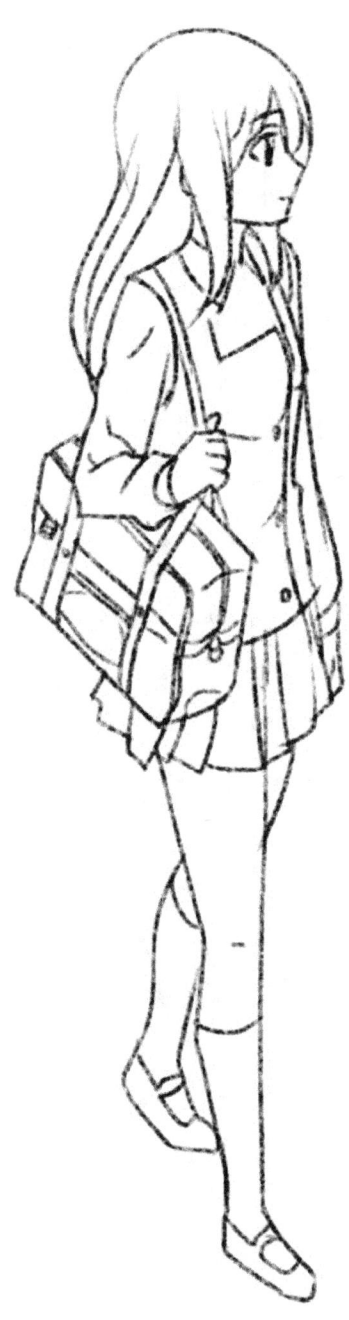

Happy Girl with Hamster

1. Draw a circle with a "t" for the face:

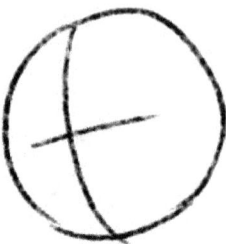

2. Draw lines to create the neck and shoulders:

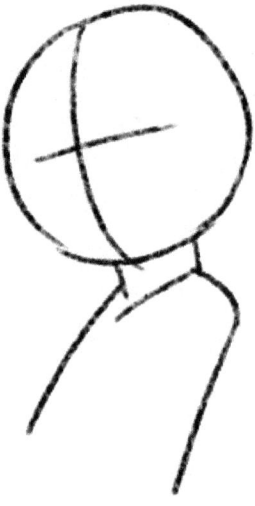

3. Connect lines in a triangle shape to the shoulder to make the torso:

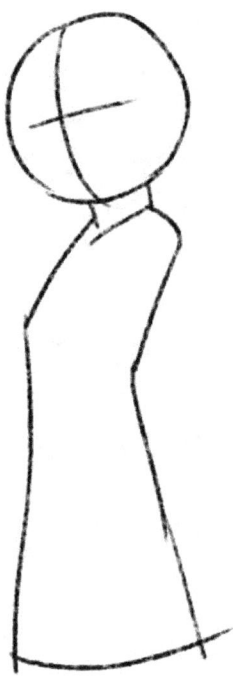

4. Make a "V" shape to make the arm. Outline the hand:

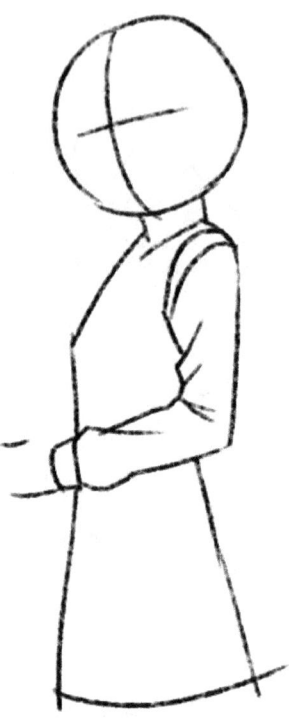

5. Draw long curved lines for legs:

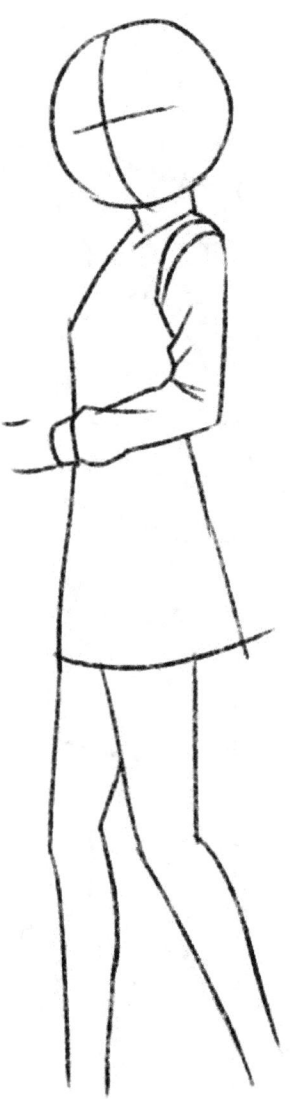

6. Use oval and triangle shapes to make the hamster. Outline the skirt:

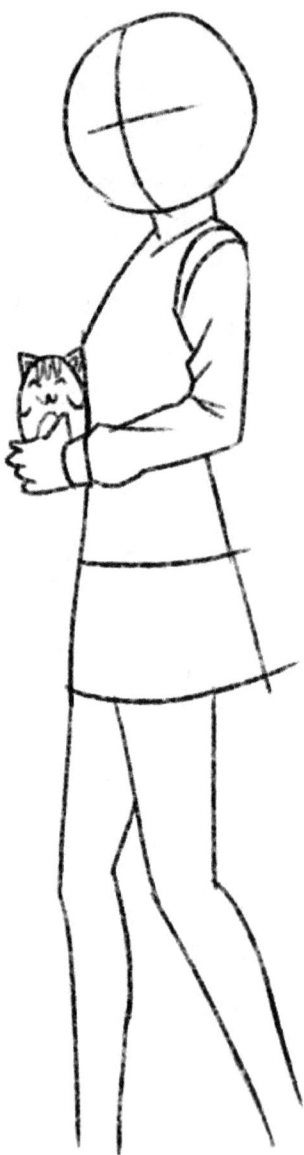

7. Add small dots and lines to detail the clothing:

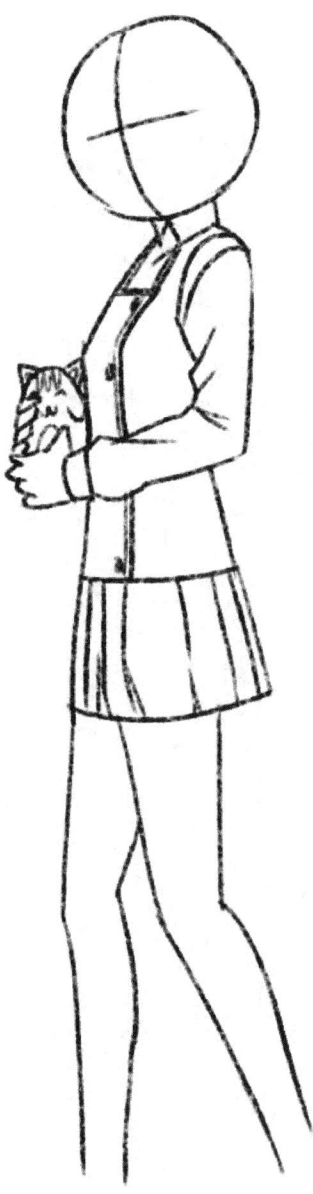

8. Use jagged lines to form the hair:

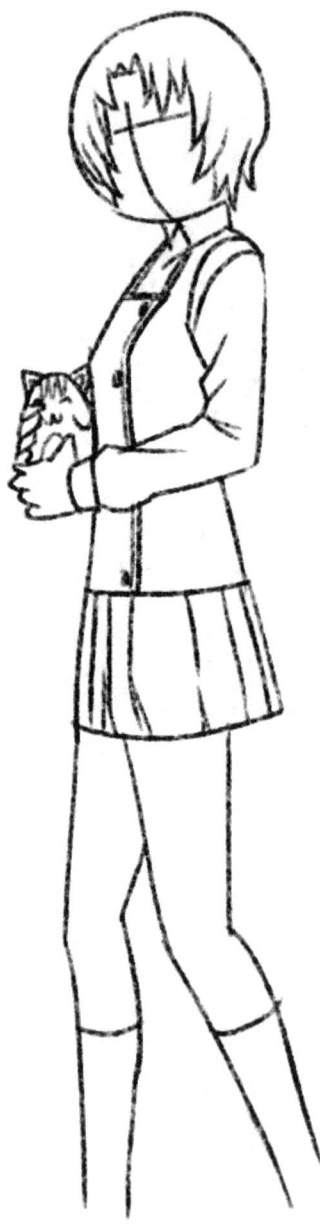

9. Draw the facial details:

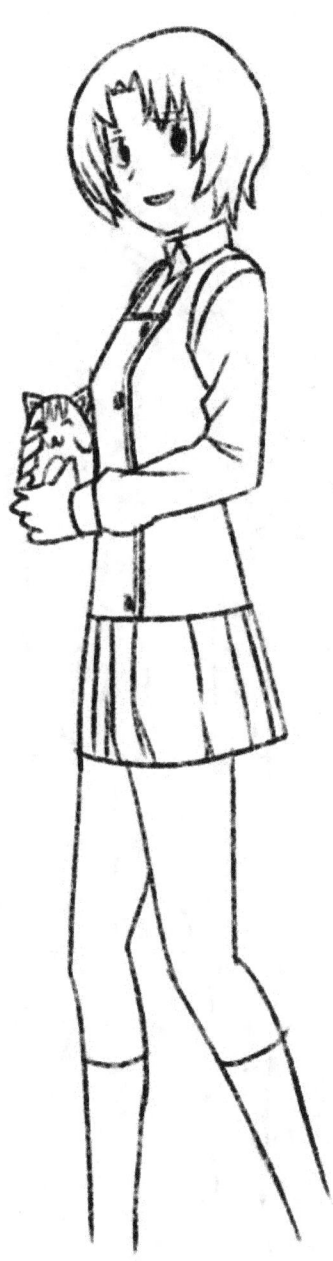

10. Use oval and square shapes to make the shoes:

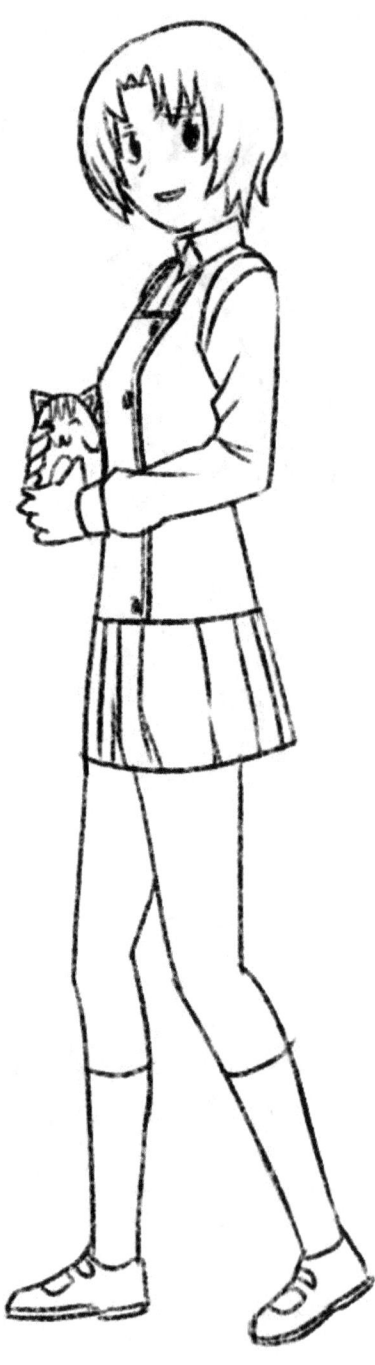

Rushed Man

1. Draw a curved line to form the spine:

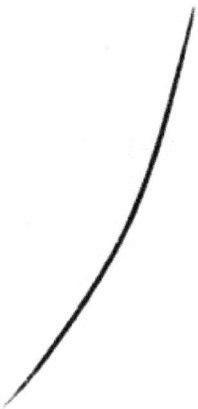

2. Draw a circle for the head. Draw line to outline the shoulders and torso:

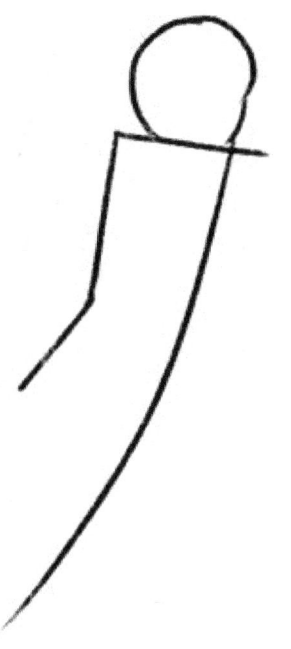

3. Draw curved lines to outline the legs:

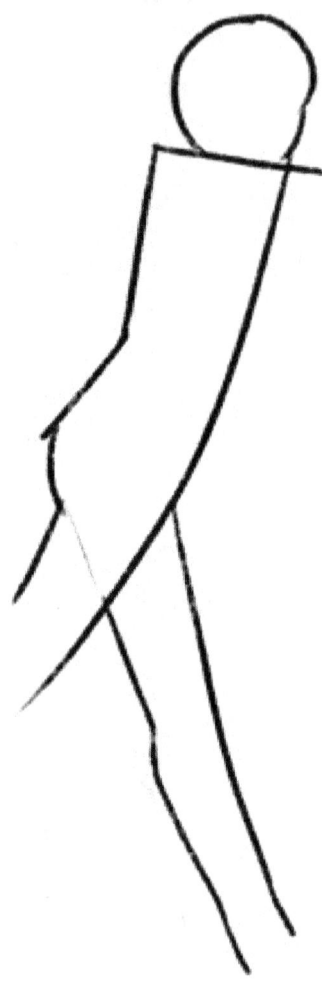

4. Add more lines to finish the legs. Add oval shapes for the feet:

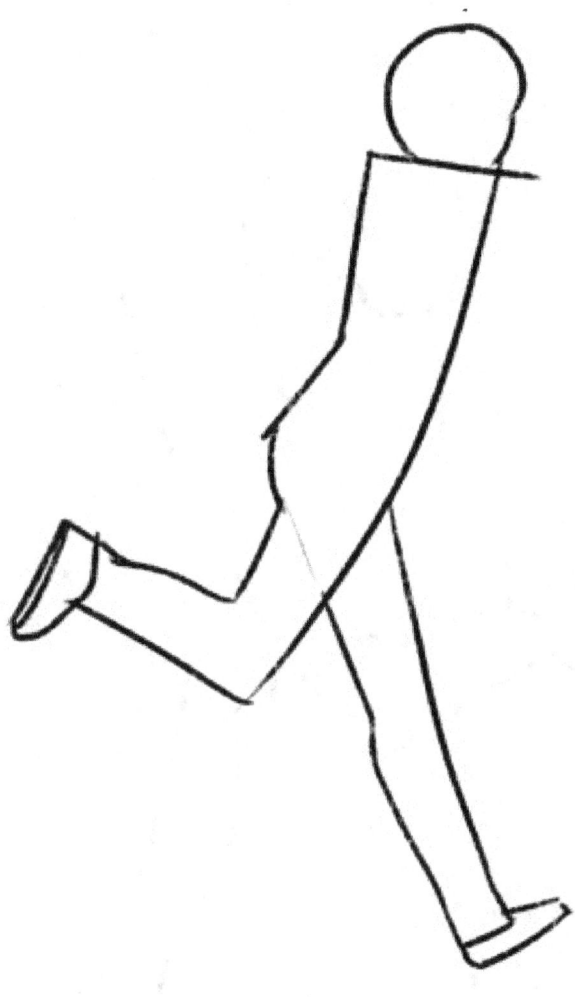

5. Draw the arms and hand using sharp lines and a circle:

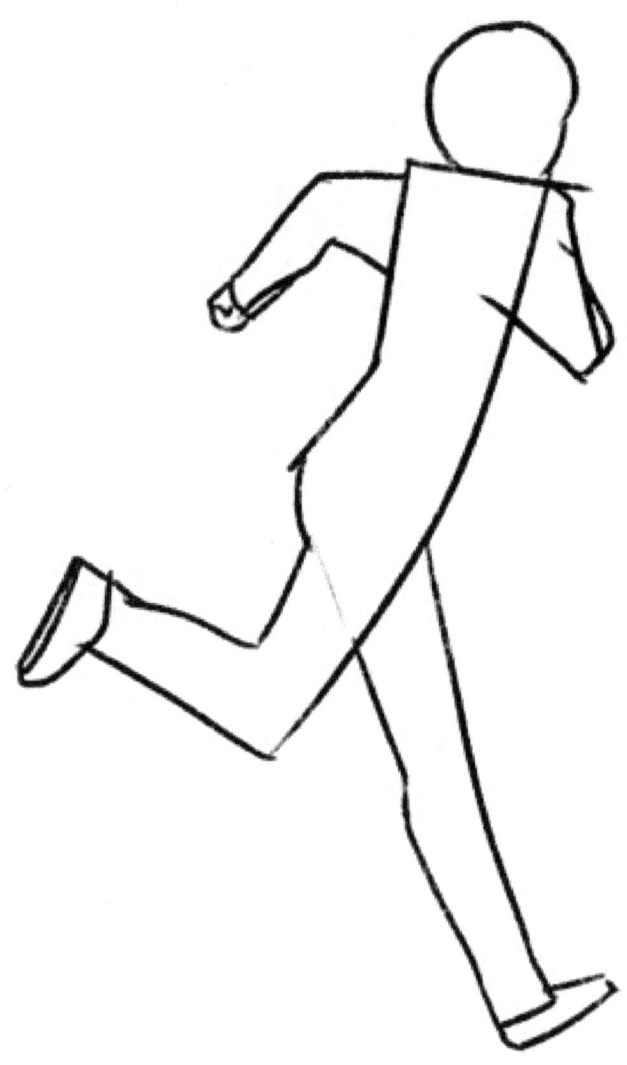

6. Using a wide triangle shape, outline the jacket:

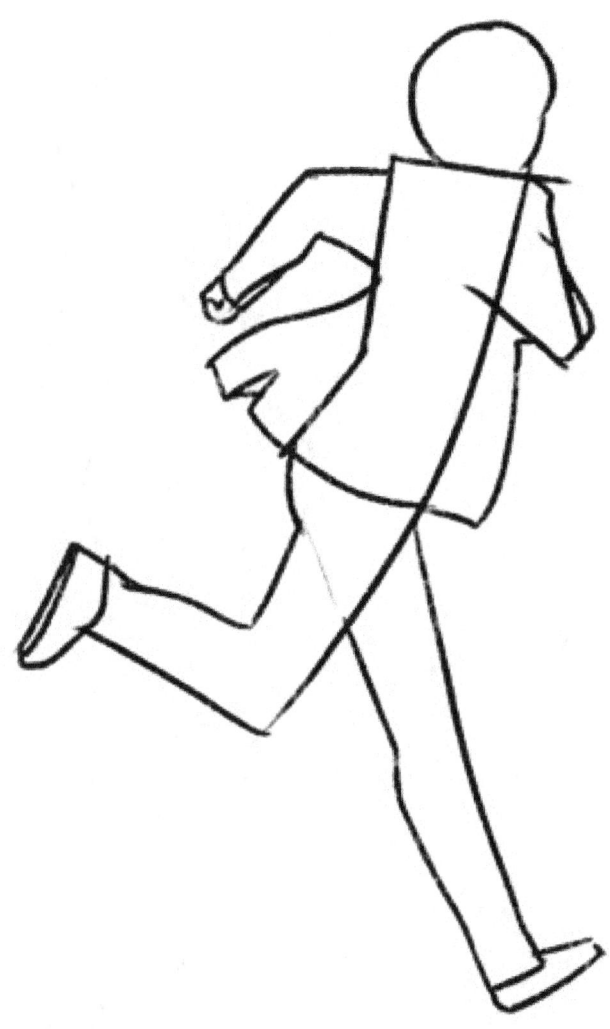

7. Draw a rectangle shape to make the bag. Add thin lines for the strap:

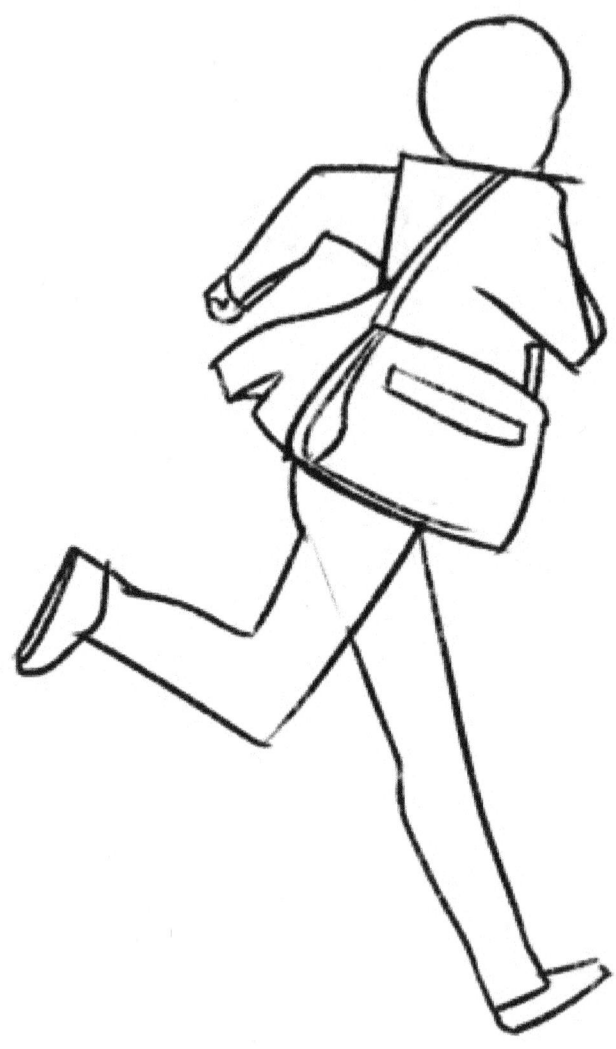

8. Draw arcs to make bag handles:

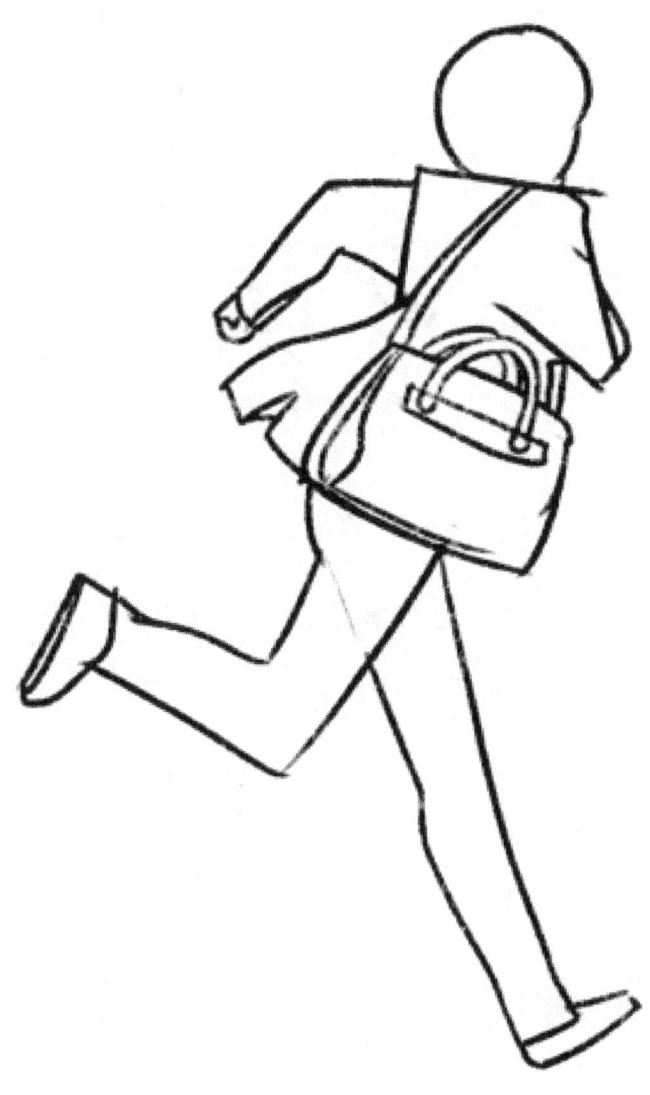

9. Draw sharp lines to make the hair:

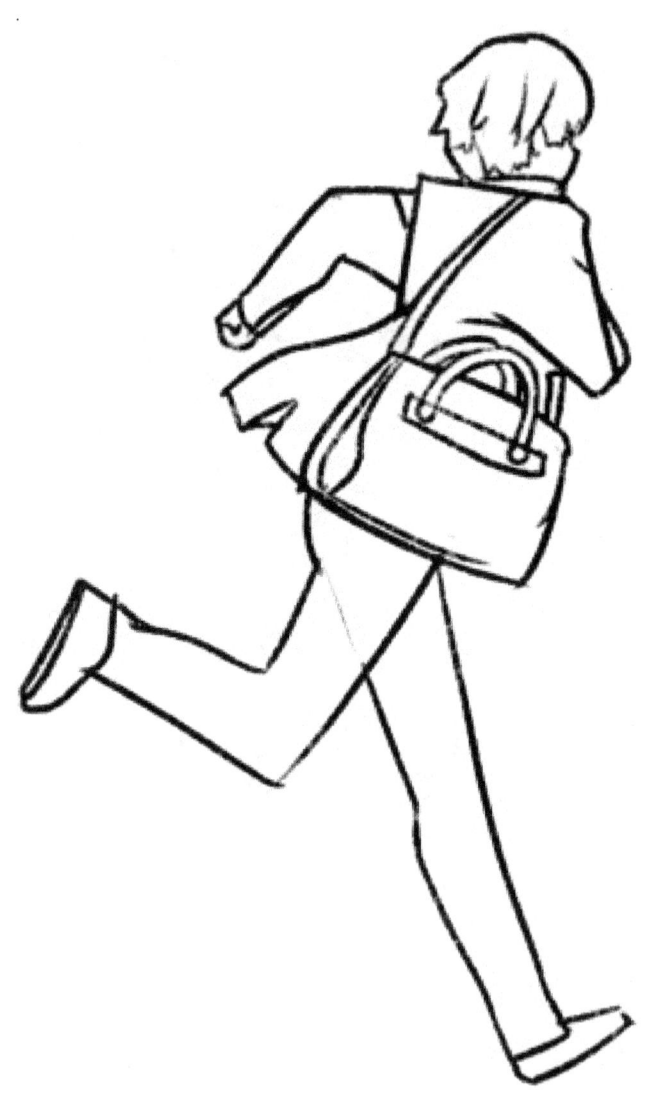

10. Draw lines to detail the shoes:

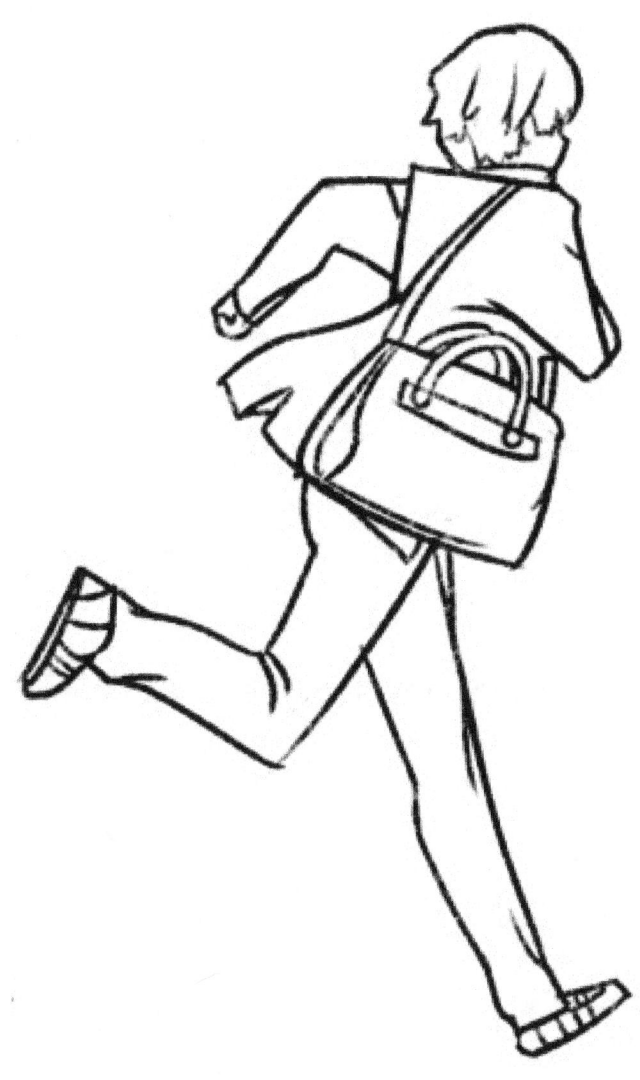

Part 5: Static Poses

Thinking Girl

1. Draw a hook shape for the hair outline and draw a "V" shape for the jaw:

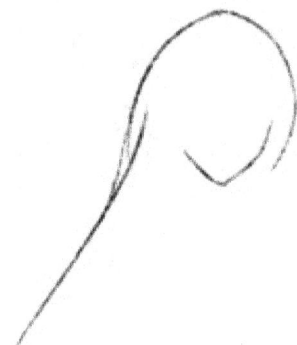

2. Draw lines for the neck and shoulders. Add curved lines for the torso:

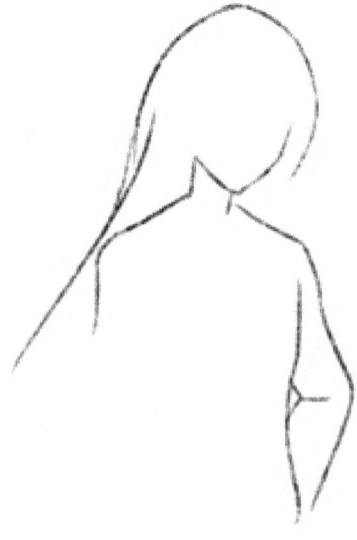

3. Draw lines for the arms and hand:

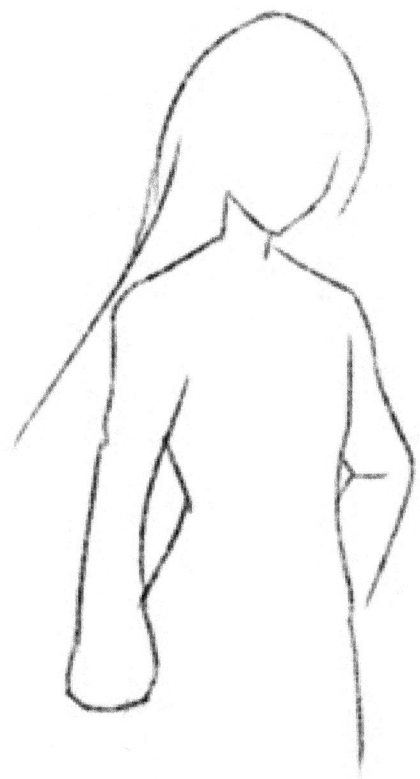

4. Draw lines to outline the legs:

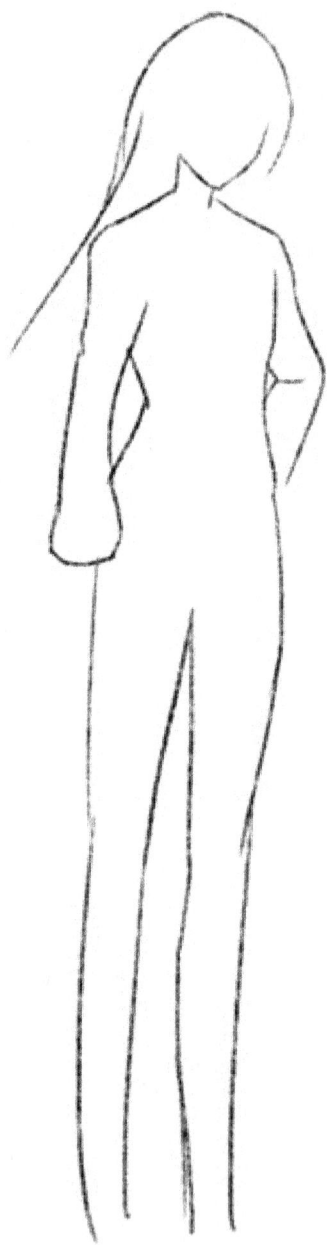

5. Draw the jacket, paying attention to the sharp angles at the waist. Draw the skirt:

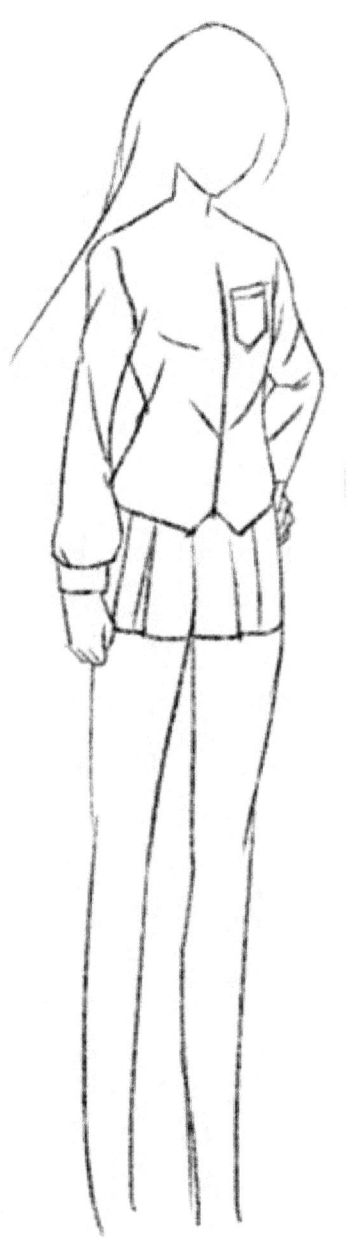

6. Draw sharp lines and pints to make the hair:

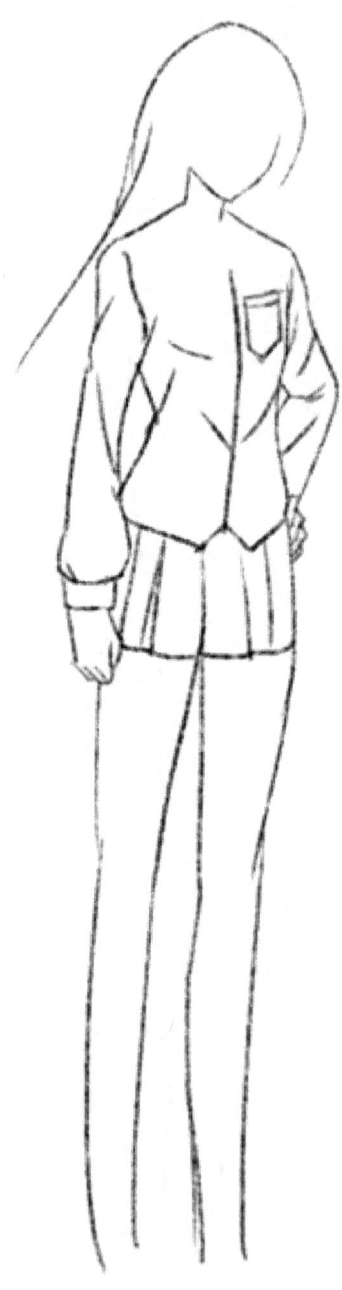

7. Draw dark lines and circles to create facial features. Draw rectangle lines for leggings:

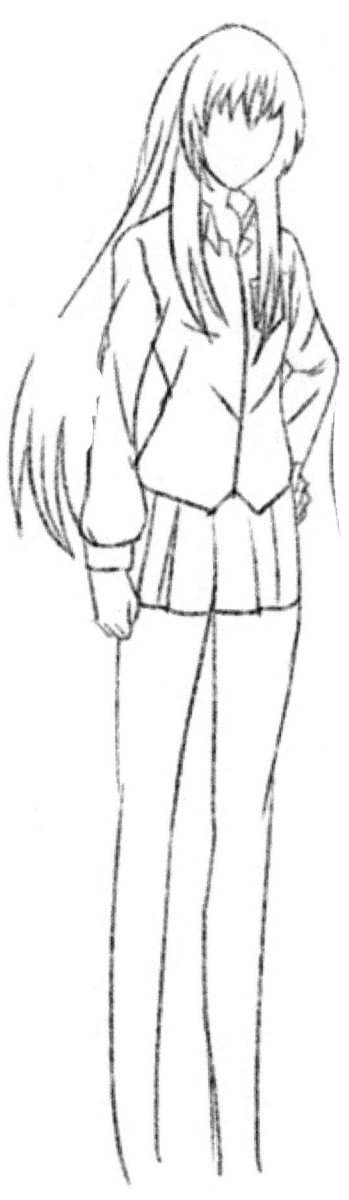

8. Draw ovals with small triangles to make the shoes:

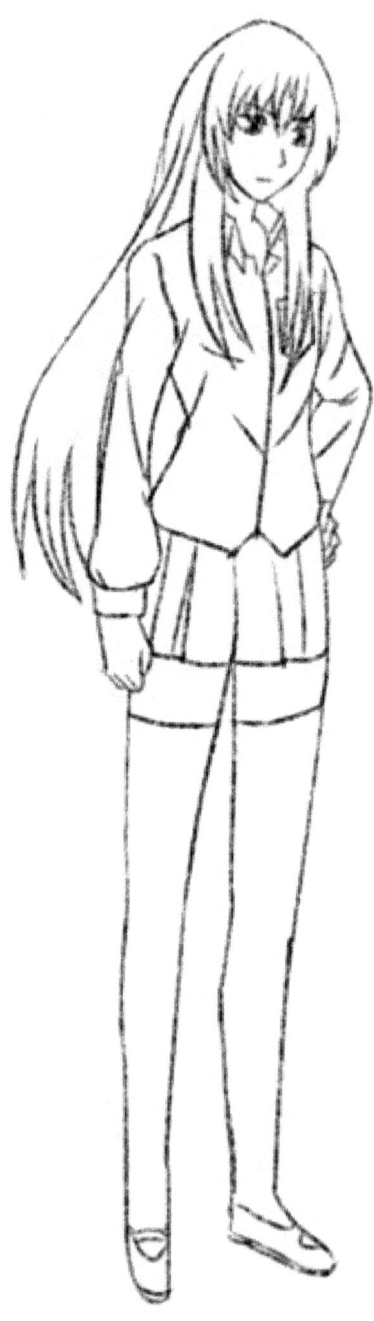

Hesitant Young Girl

1. Draw a circle for the head:

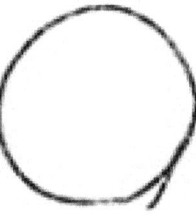

2. Draw lines to create the outline for the spine, torso and shoulders:

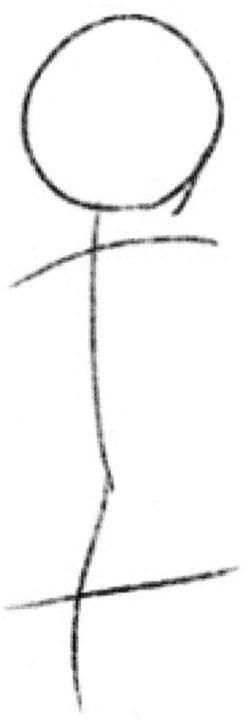

3. Create triangle like lines to form the neck and torso:

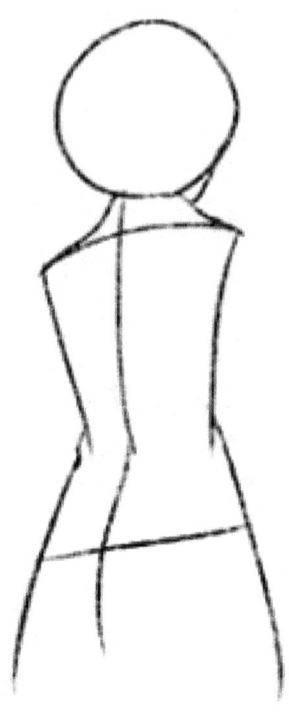

4. Draw an almond like shape where the legs will be placed:

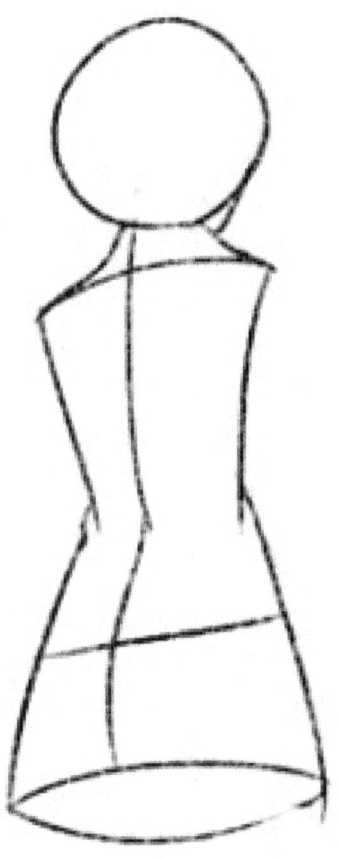

5. Draw long curving lines to form the legs:

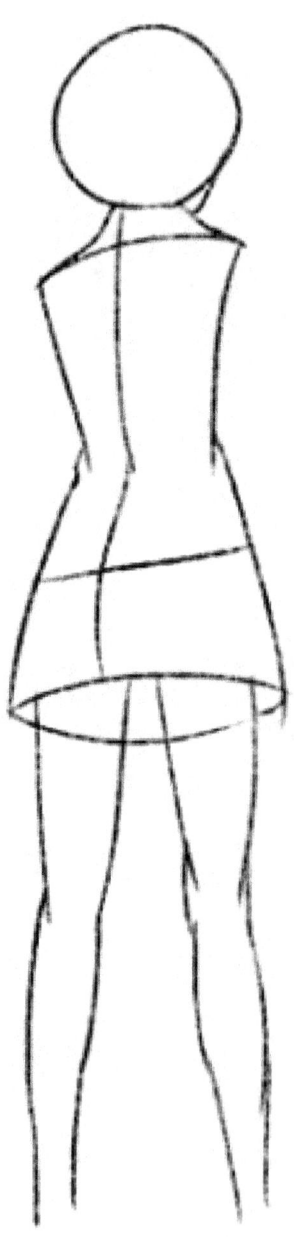

6. Draw lines to form the arm:

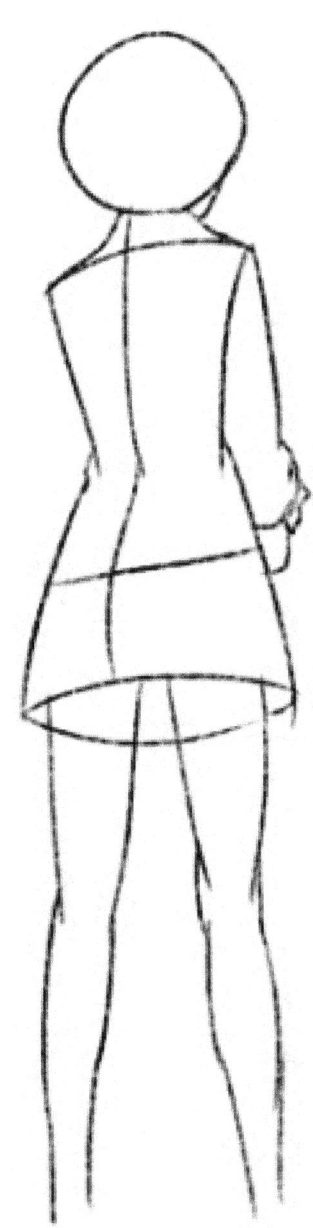

7. Draw lines to contour the shirt:

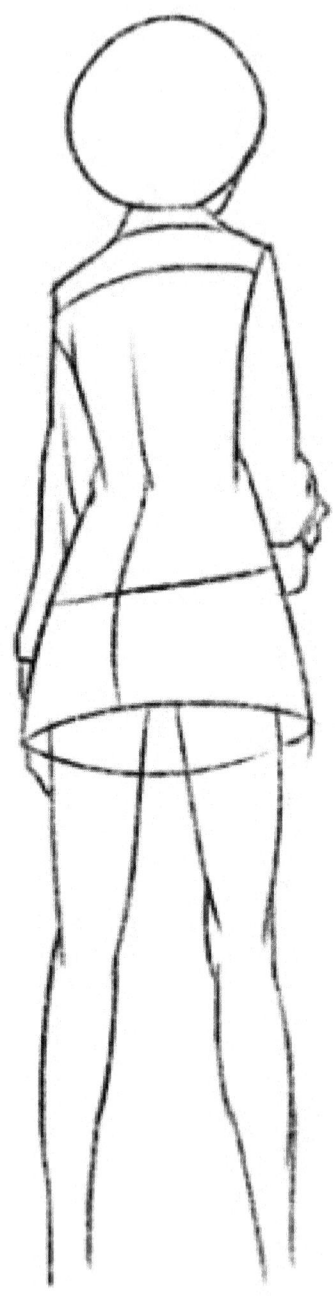

8. Add wrinkle lines to detail the shirt:

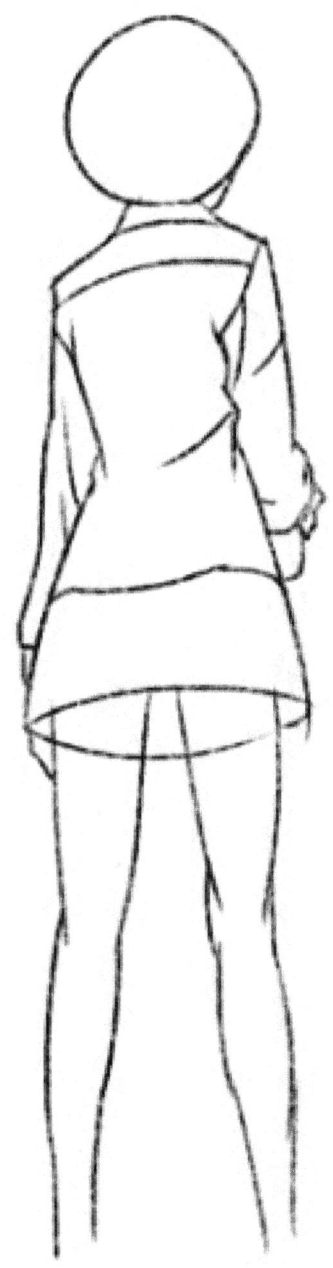

9. Add lines to detail the skirt:

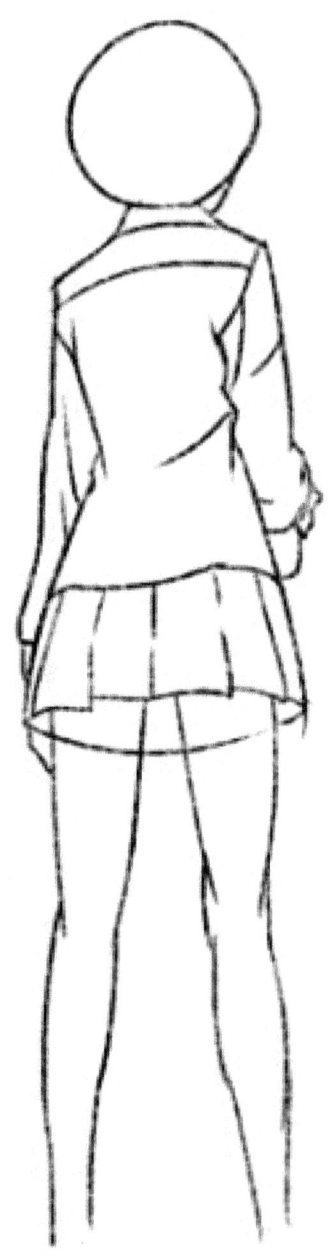

10. Draw oval like shapes to form the feet:

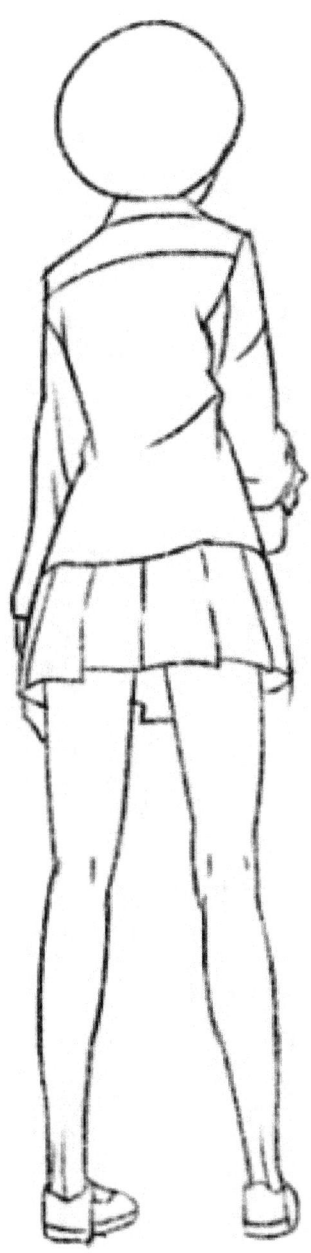

11. Use jagged lines and pints to create hair:

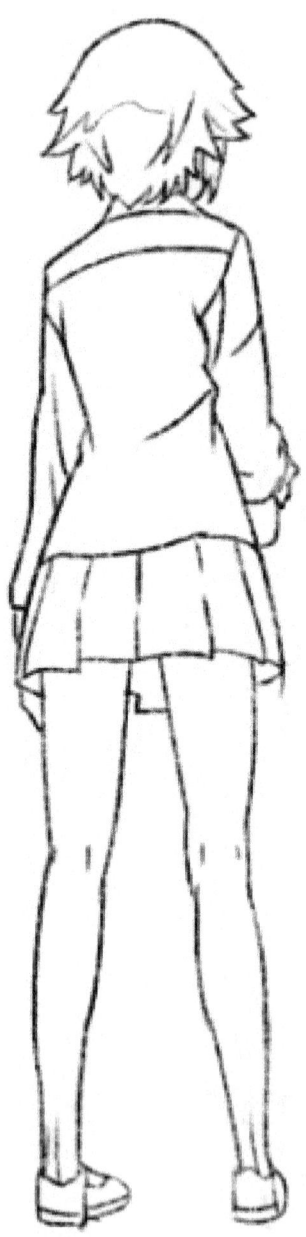

Relaxed Girl

1. Draw an upside down "U" shape for the hair line:

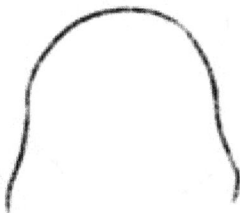

2. Draw a circle for the head. Draw lines to outline the neck and shoulders:

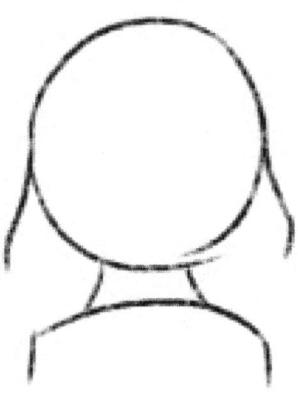

3. Draw a long shape to form the torso. Draw lines down the center to detail the shirt:

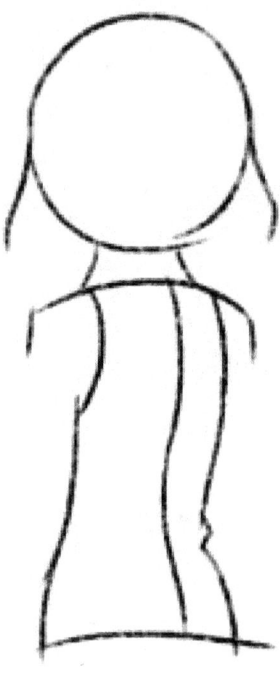

4. Draw a square like shape for the skirt. Add lines to form wrinkles:

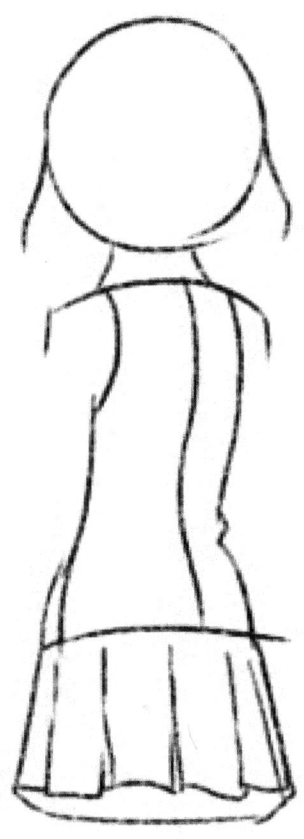

5. Draw lines for the arms and legs:

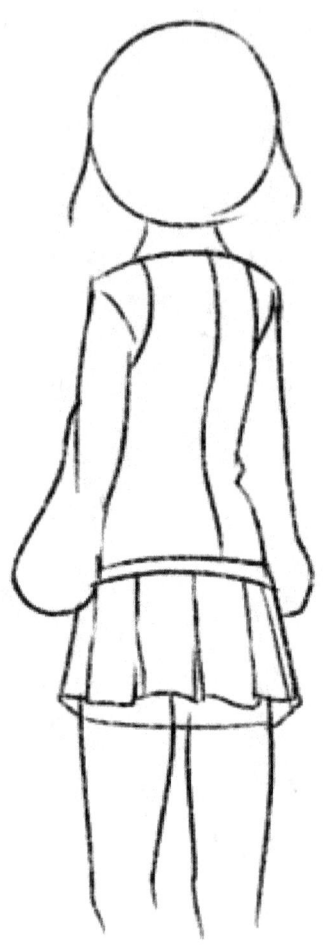

6. Use sharp pints for the hair. Draw the hands:

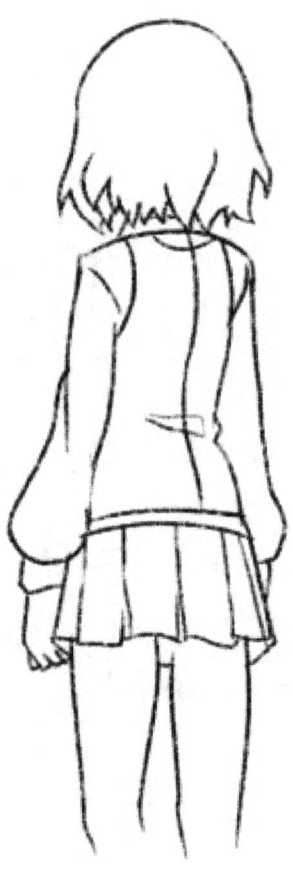

7. Finish the legs and draw triangle shapes to make shoes:

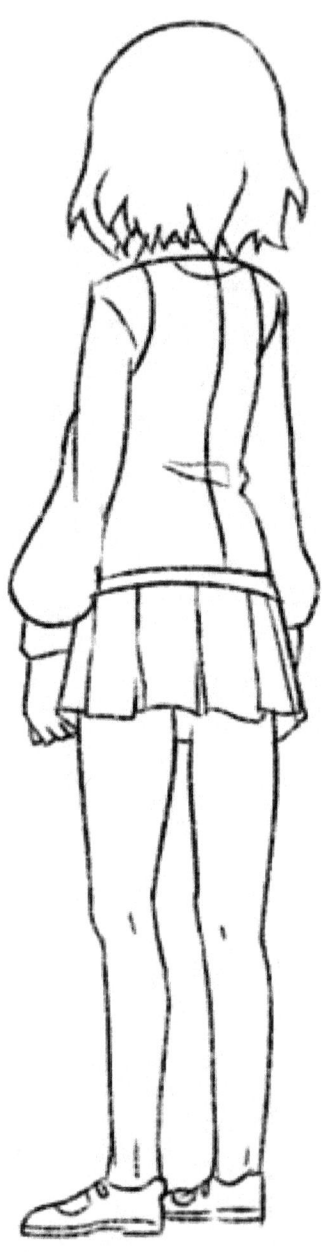

Defeated Man

1. Draw a line to form the spine:

2. Draw square shapes and a thin line to outline the body and head:

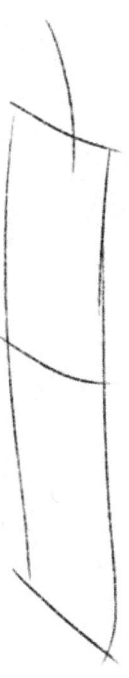

3. Draw an upside down tear for the head. Draw lines to create shoulders and facial feature guidelines:

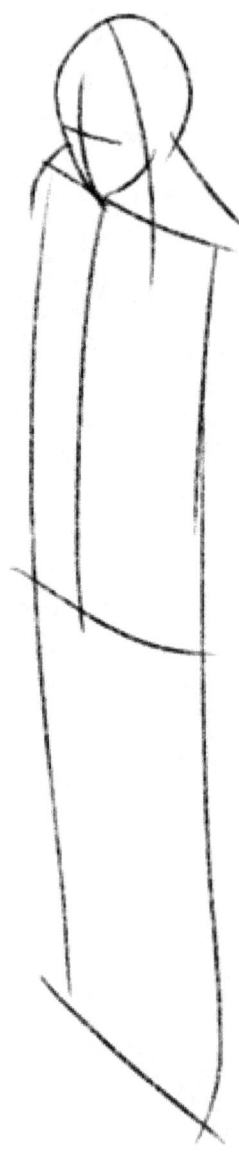

4. Contour the torso. Add lines for the shirt. Draw lines for the book and right leg and arm:

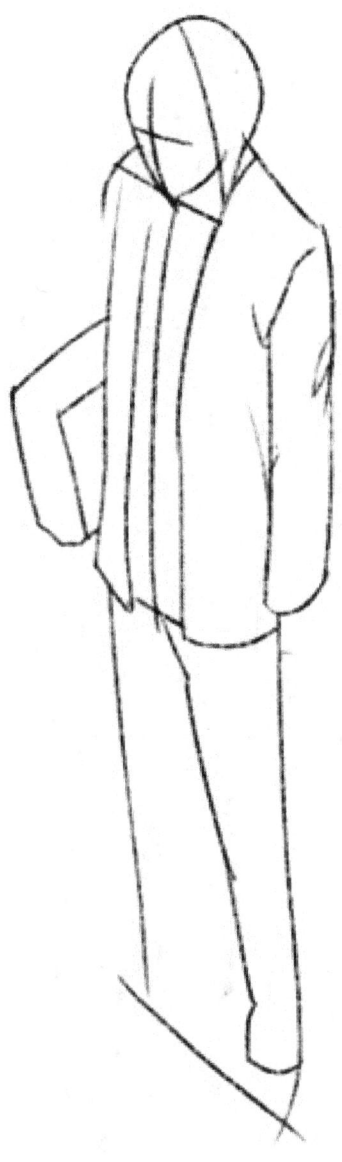

5. Draw the other leg. Add small lines for knees:

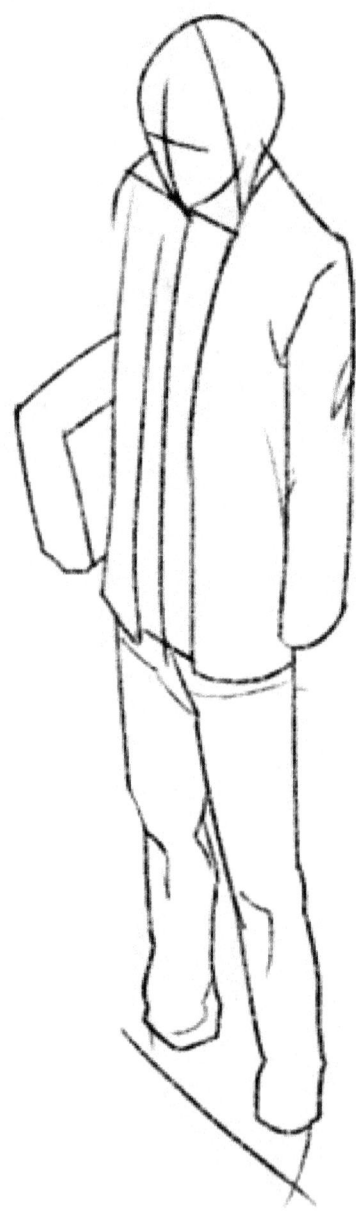

6. Draw details for the clothing. Make the hand:

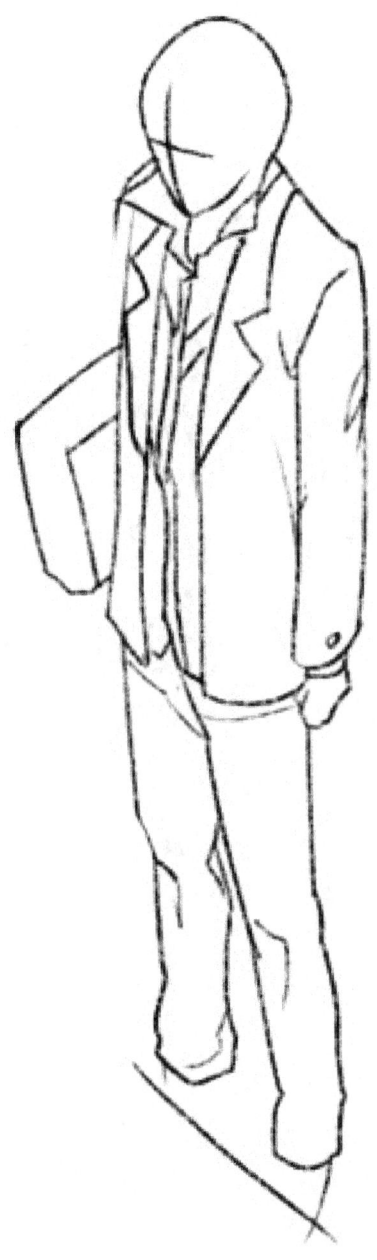

7. Add lines and rectangle shapes to put details on the book:

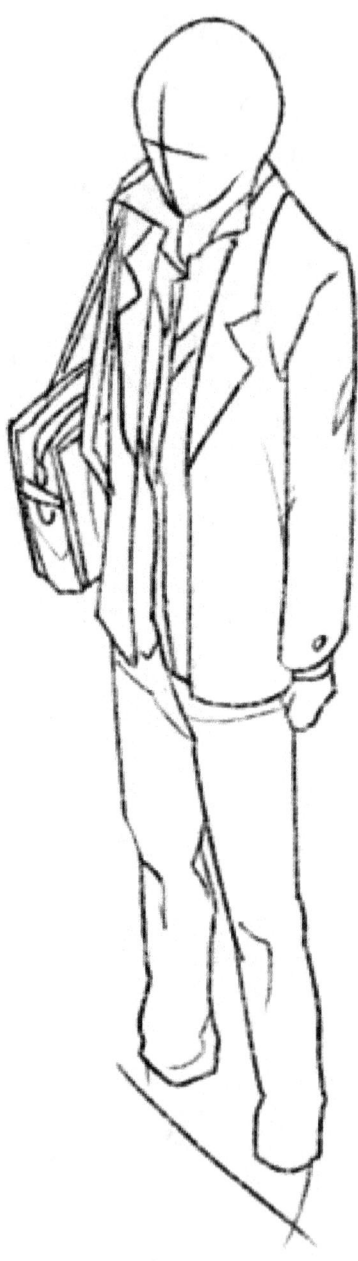

8. Draw feet with ovals and rectangle shapes:

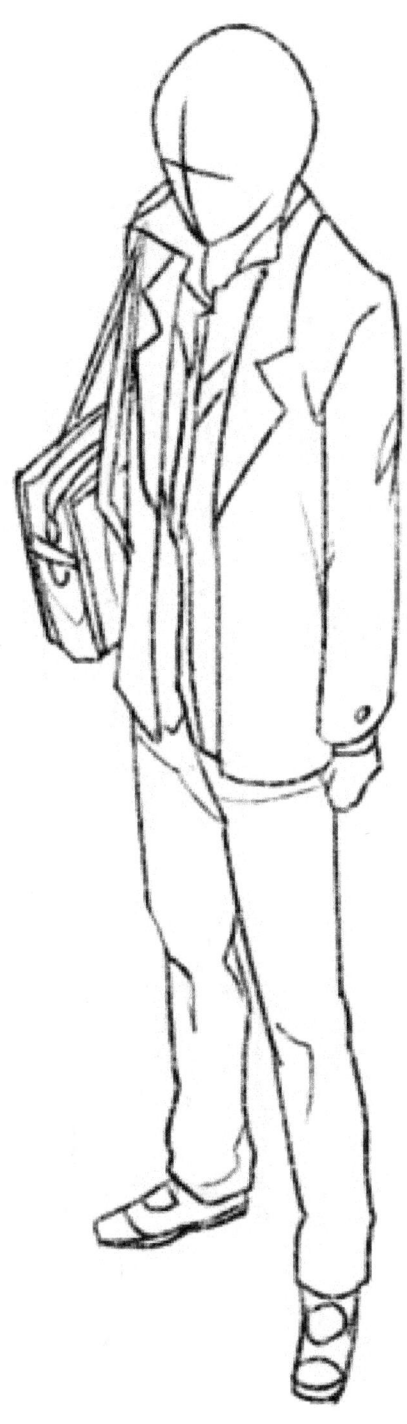

9. Draw facial features using small lines. Draw the hair:

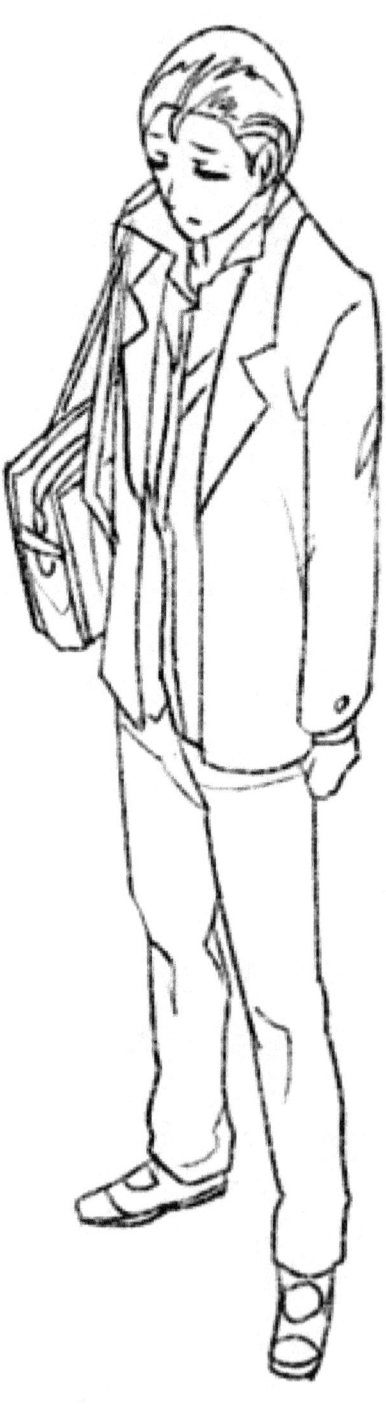

Part 6: Dynamic Poses

Fighting Woman

1. Draw "V" shapes for the hair and jaw outlines. Add a "T" shape for face guidelines:

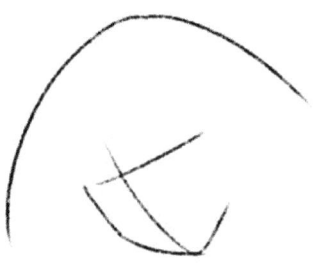

2. Draw loose long lines and sharp pointed lines to create the hair:

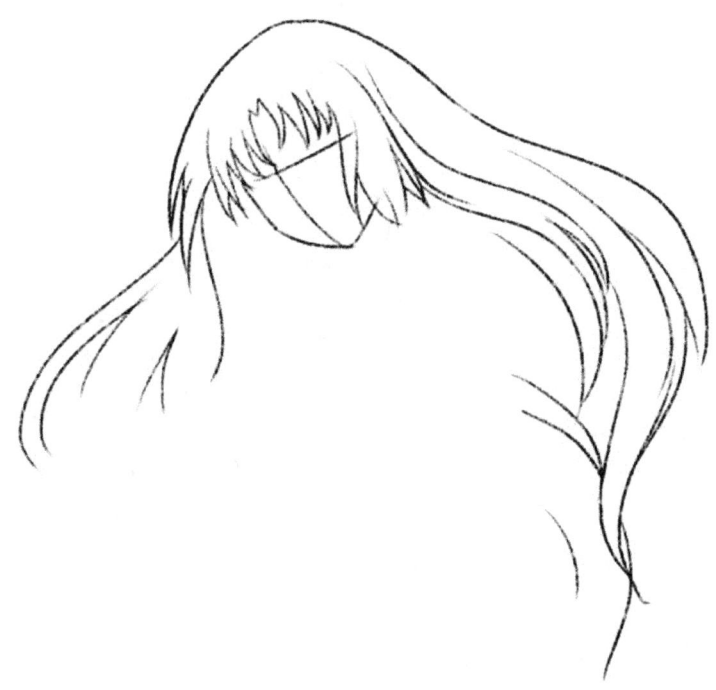

3. Draw lines to form the right shoulder:

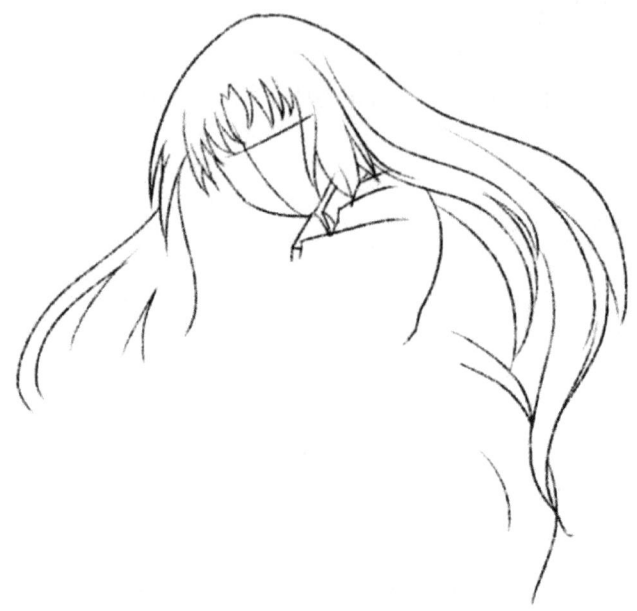

4. Add more lines to detail the arm:

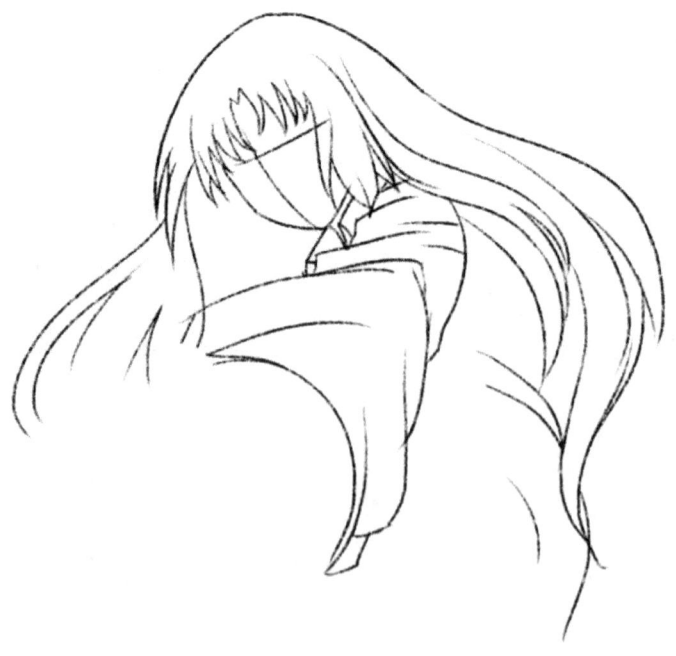

5. Draw the left hand with square shapes and lines. Begin the outline of the torso:

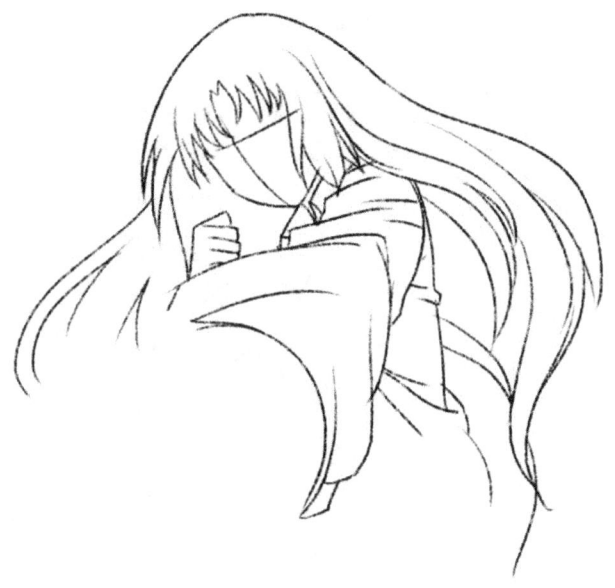

6. Finish the torso:

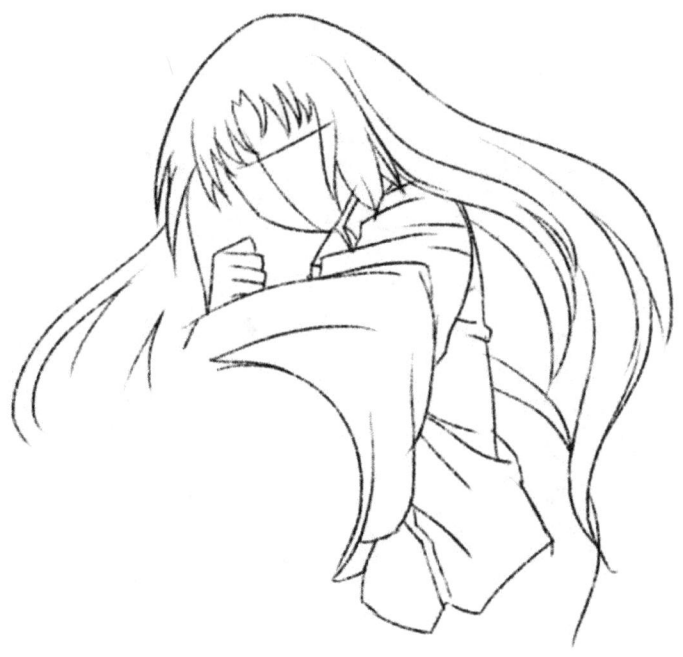

7. Draw the skirt using a triangle shape:

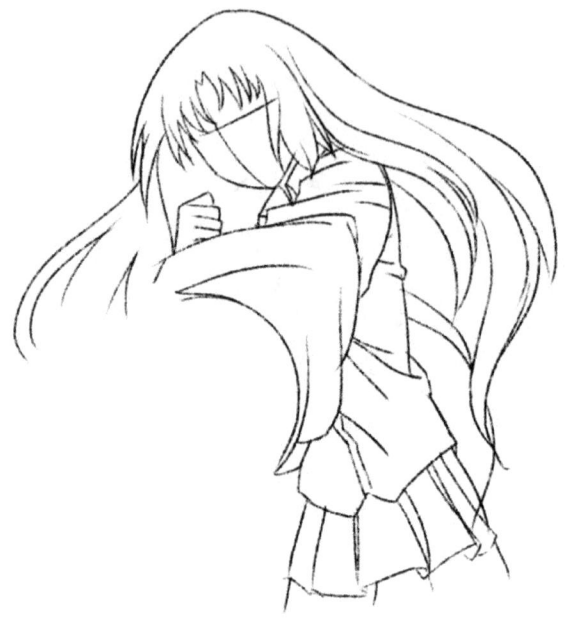

8. Draw the outline of the fist:

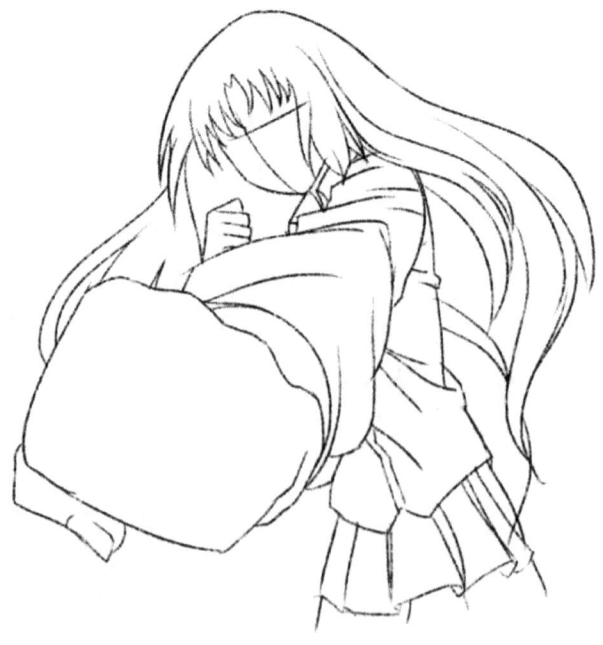

9. Draw the fingers and contour the fist:

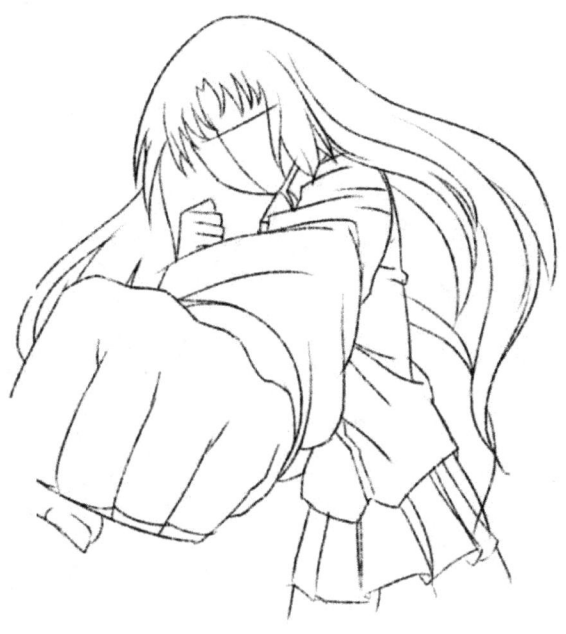

10. Draw action lines on the fist:

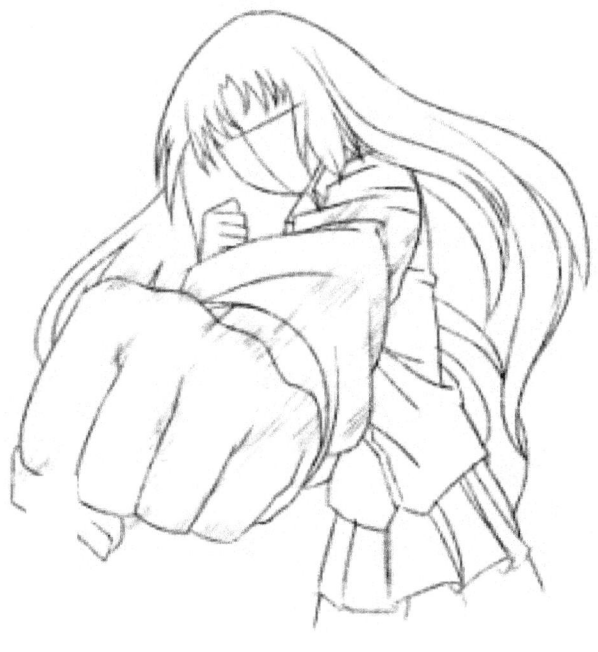

11. Draw facial features using dark lines, circles, and square shapes:

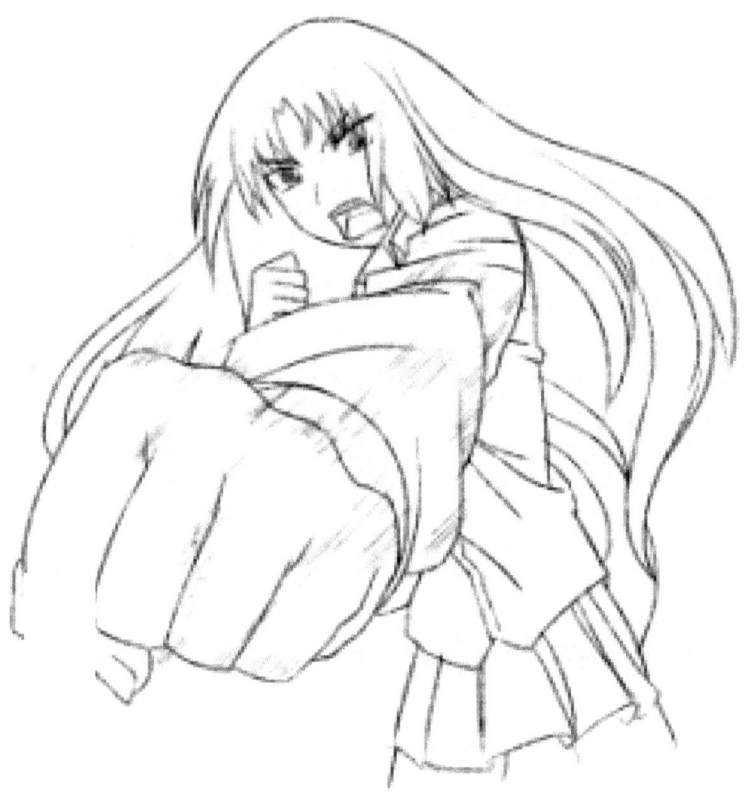

Defensive Girl

1. Draw a "C" shape for the hair outline. Draw an arc for the jaw. Create a "t" shape for face guidelines:

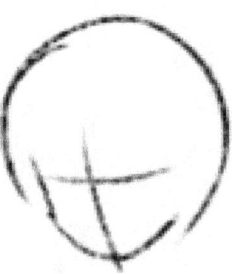

2. Form a "U" like shape for the chest and add lines for the shoulders:

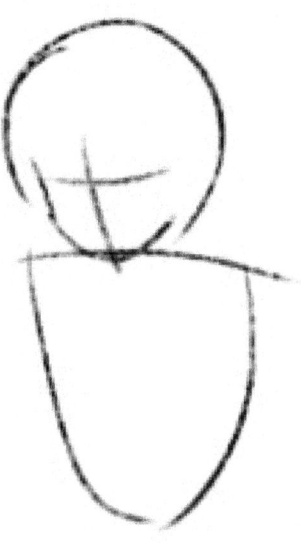

3. Draw a triangle shape for the skirt. Draw lines to form the arms and shoulders:

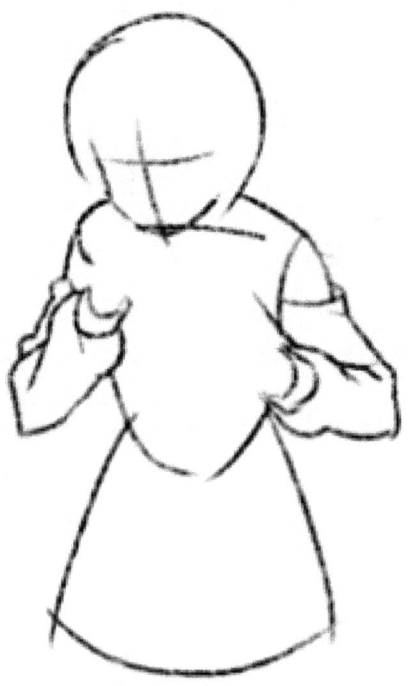

4. Draw lines to detail the shirt:

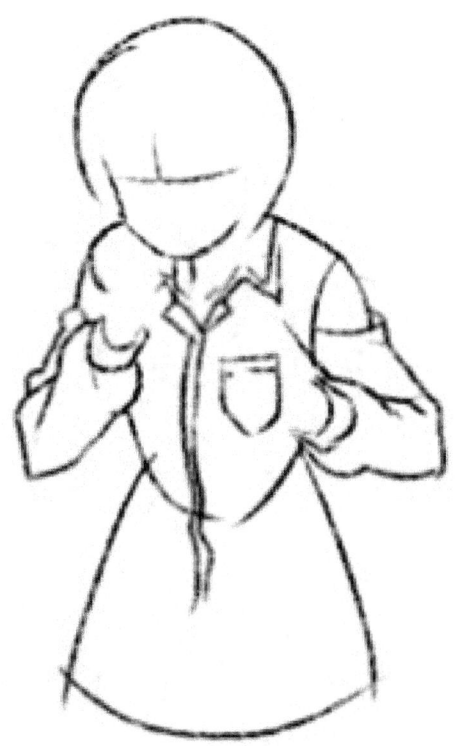

5. Draw hair using jagged lines and draw wrinkle lines in the skirt:

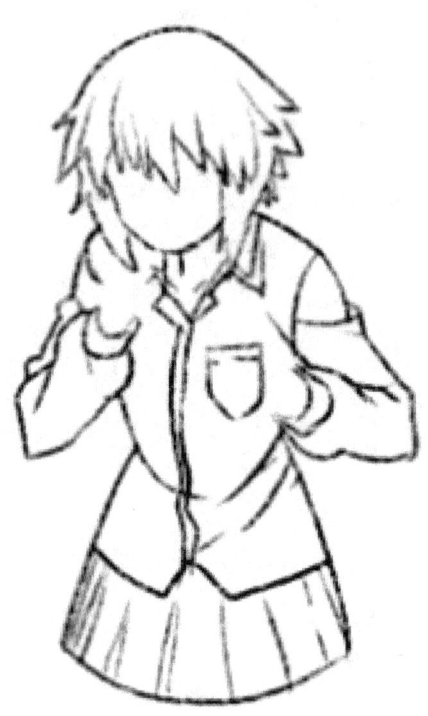

6. Draw curved lines to form legs and the feet:

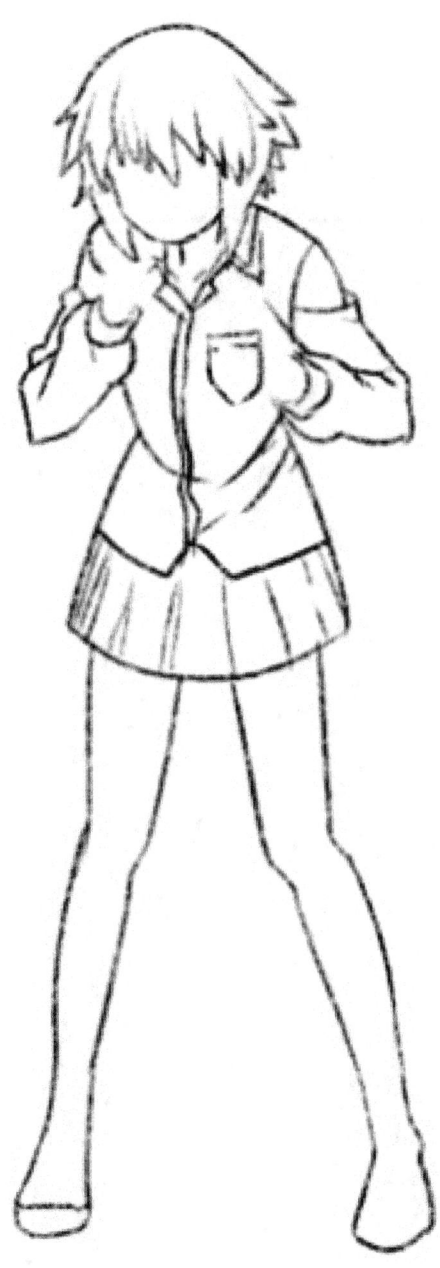

7. Add facial features using dark lines and square shapes. Use oval shapes to make shoes:

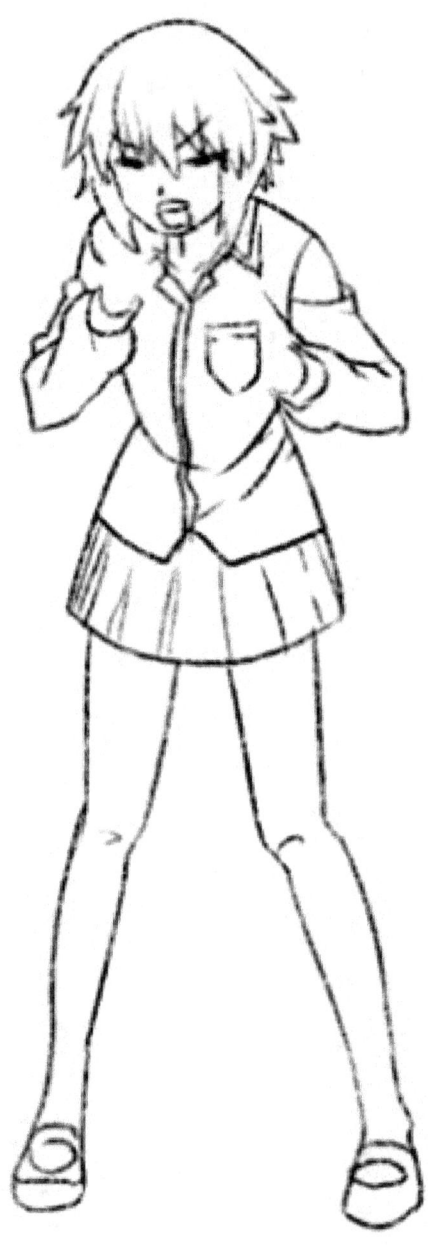

8. Draw hands and fingers:

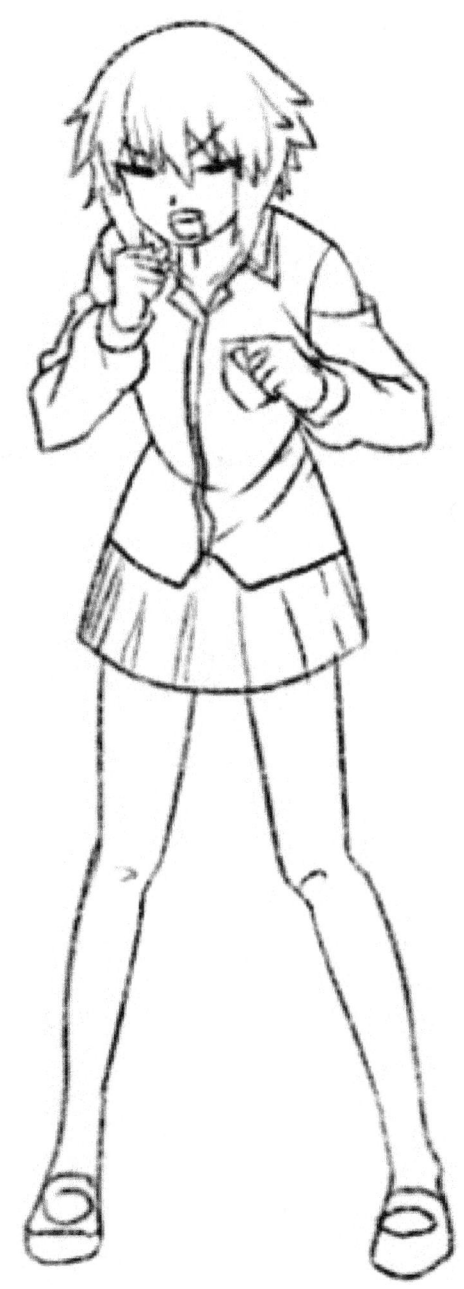

Excited Girl

1. Draw a "C" like shape for the hairline. Draw a "V' shape for the jaw line:

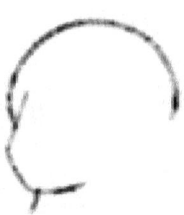

2. Draw jagged lines to form hair. Draw a rectangle and lines to begin the shirt:

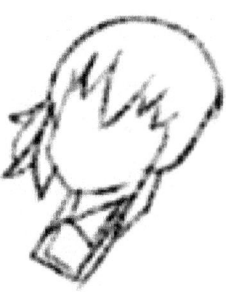

3. Draw rectangle shapes to create arms. Draw small lines to form cuffs:

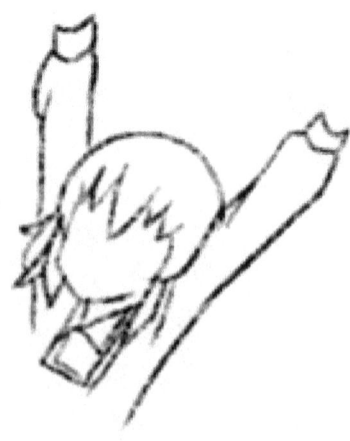

4. Add curved lines for the torso:

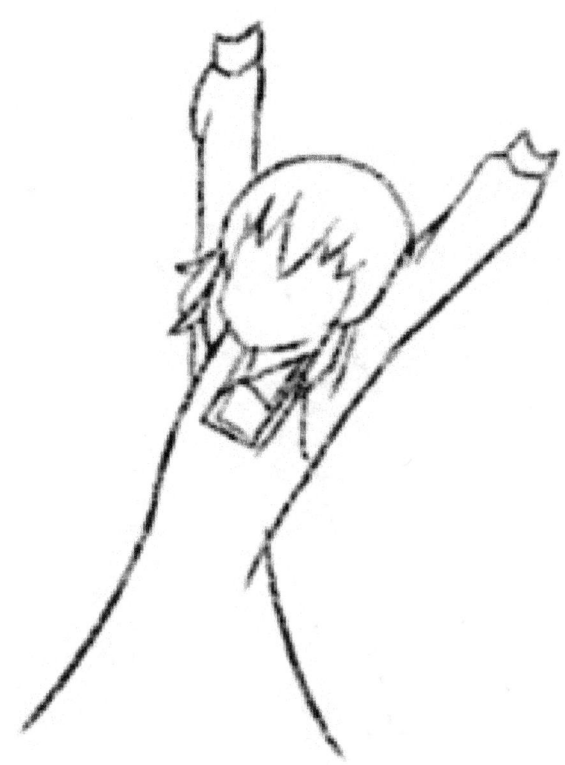

5. Draw arcs to form the skirt. Draw lines and small circles to detail the shirt:

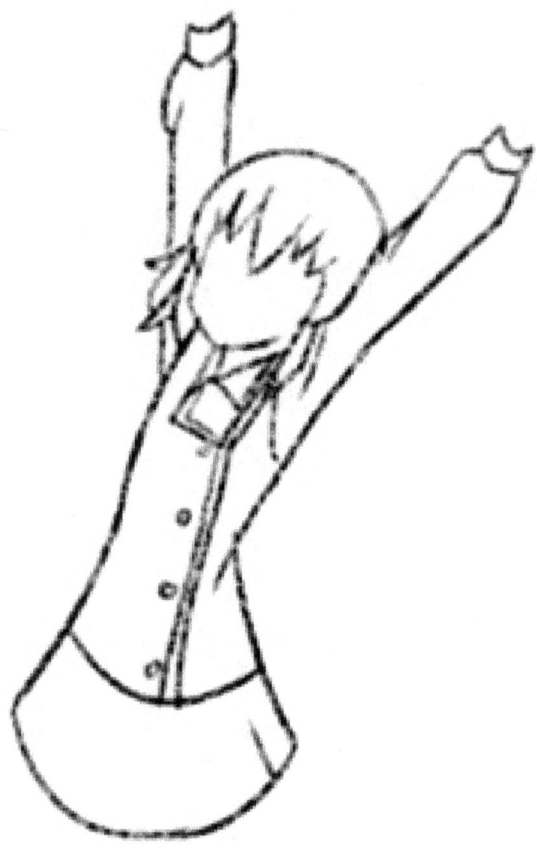

6. Draw sharp rectangle shapes to contour the skirt:

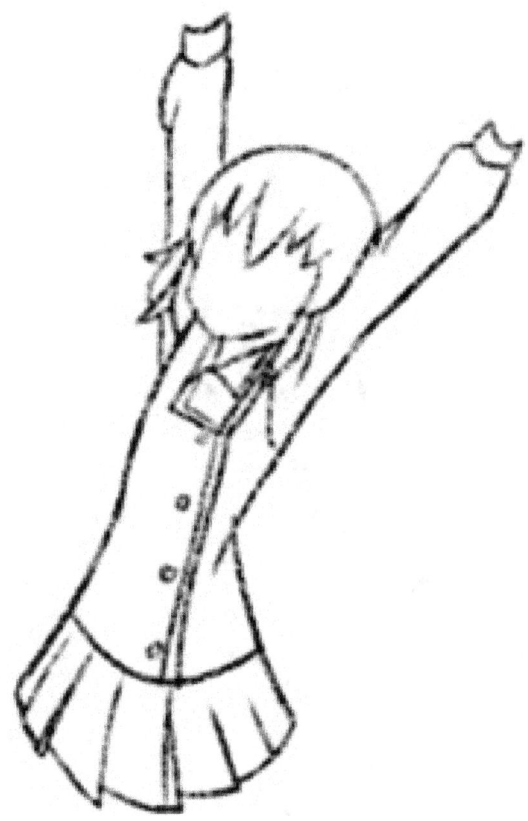

7. Add long thin lines to form legs:

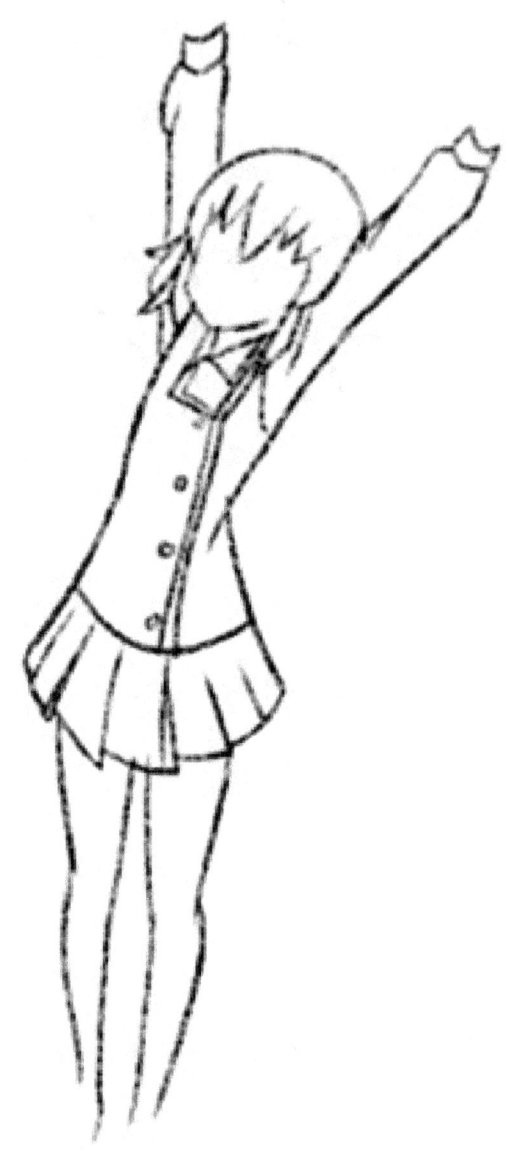

8. Draw shapes and lines to form legs:

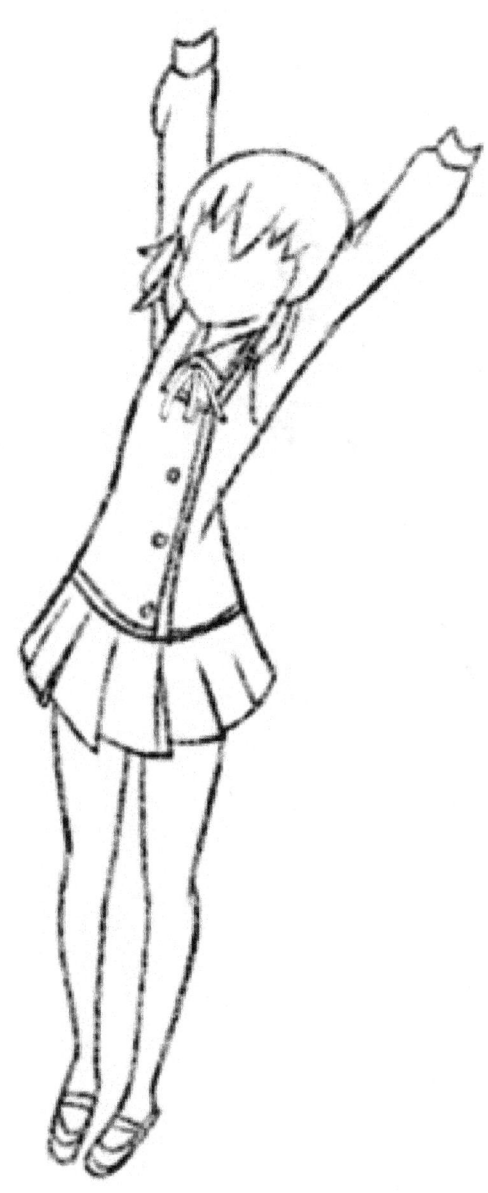

9. Draw the facial features using circles and dots:

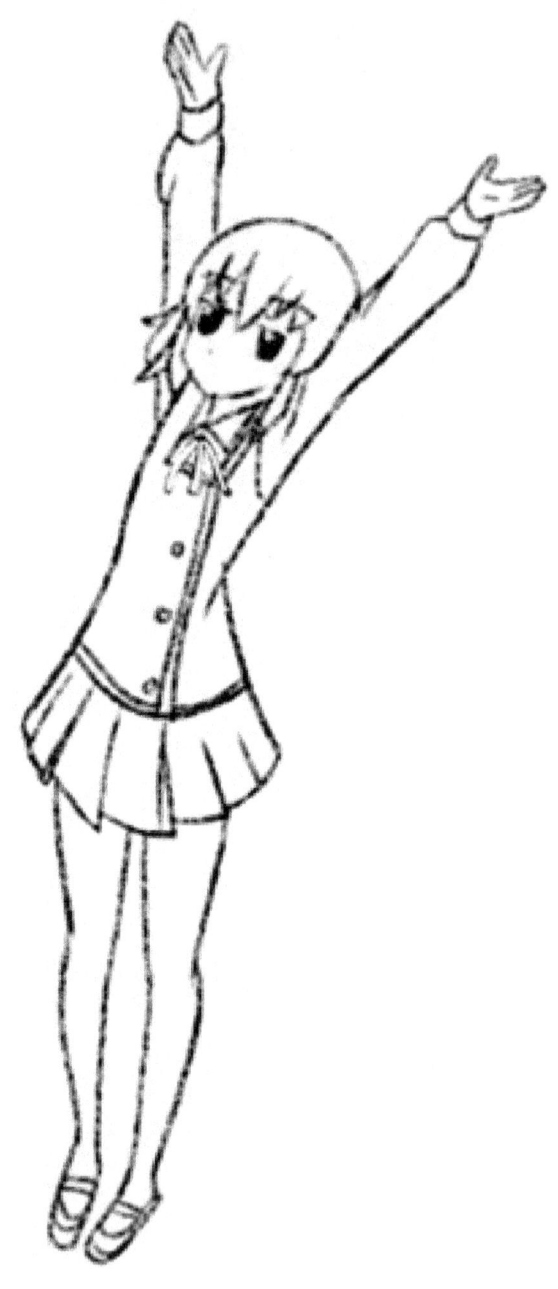

Ecstatic Boy

1. Draw "C" a shape and a "V" shape to form the hair and face outline:

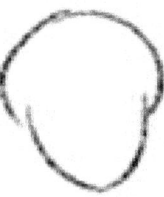

2. Draw rectangles for arms and a "t" shape for the face guidelines:

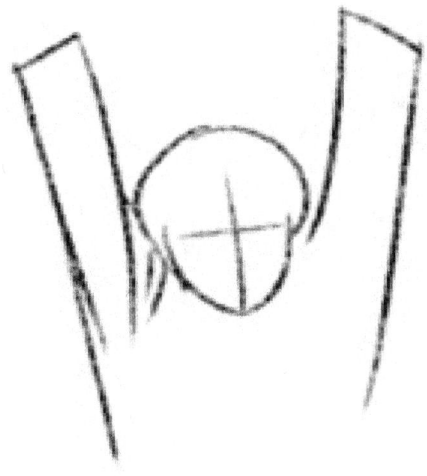

3. Draw a triangle shape for the torso:

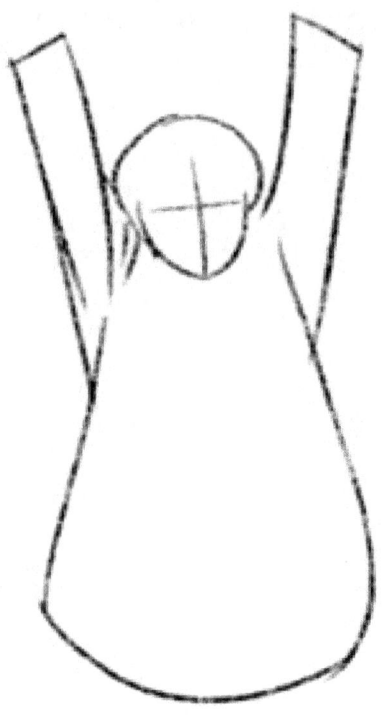

4. Draw the right leg using long thin lines:

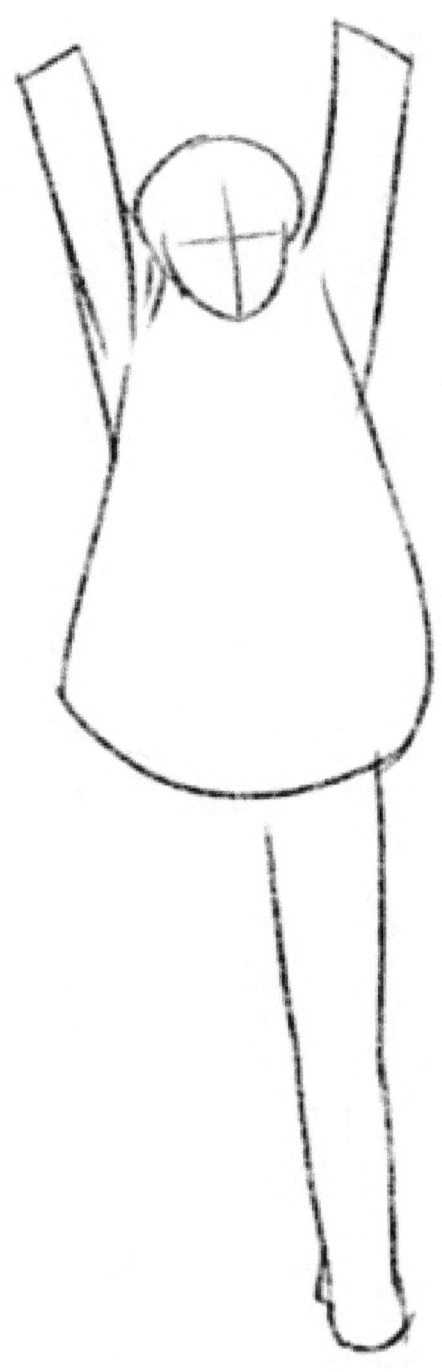

5. Draw the left leg using thin long lines:

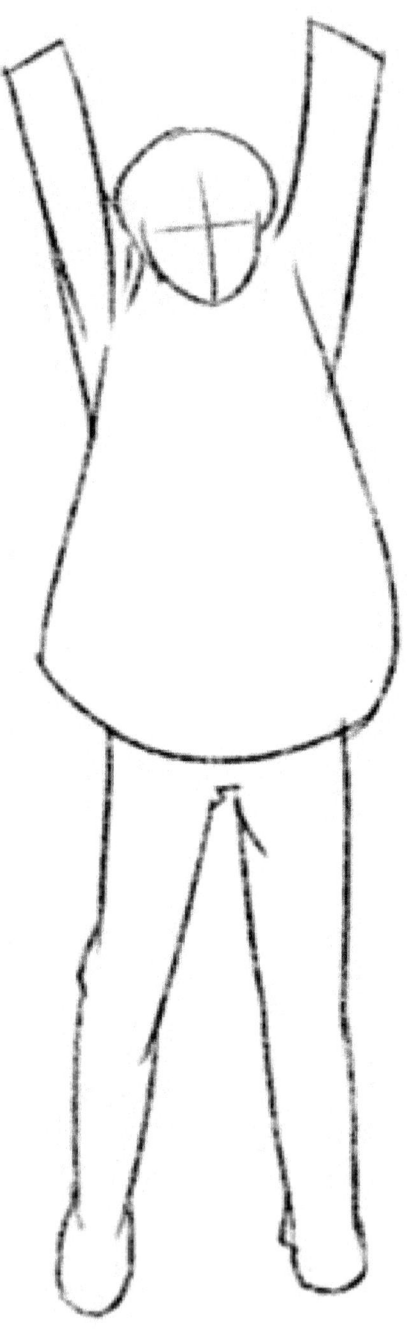

6. Using ovals and thin arcs create the shoes and outline the jacket:

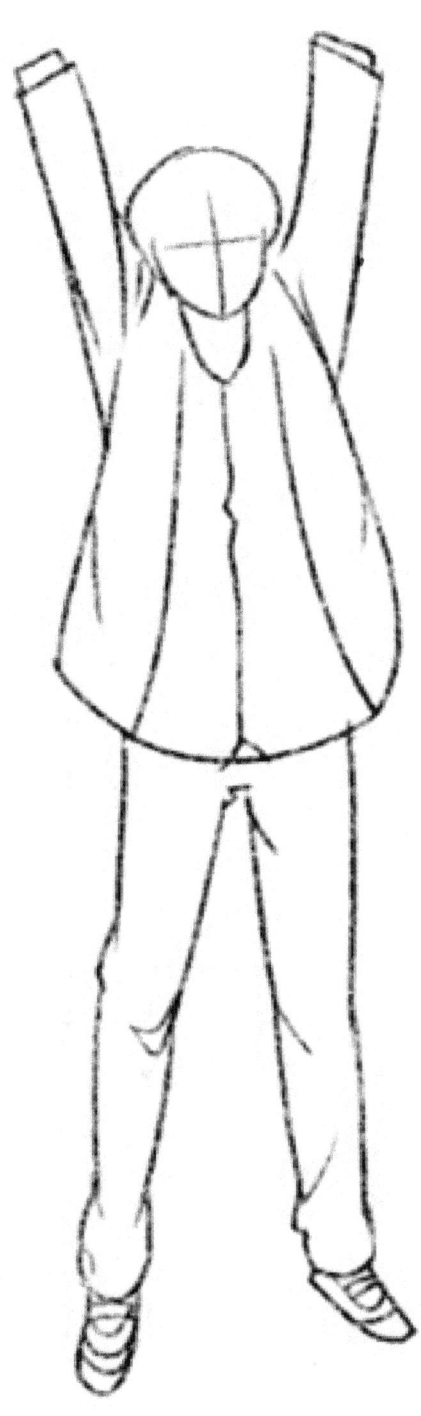

7. Add jacket details:

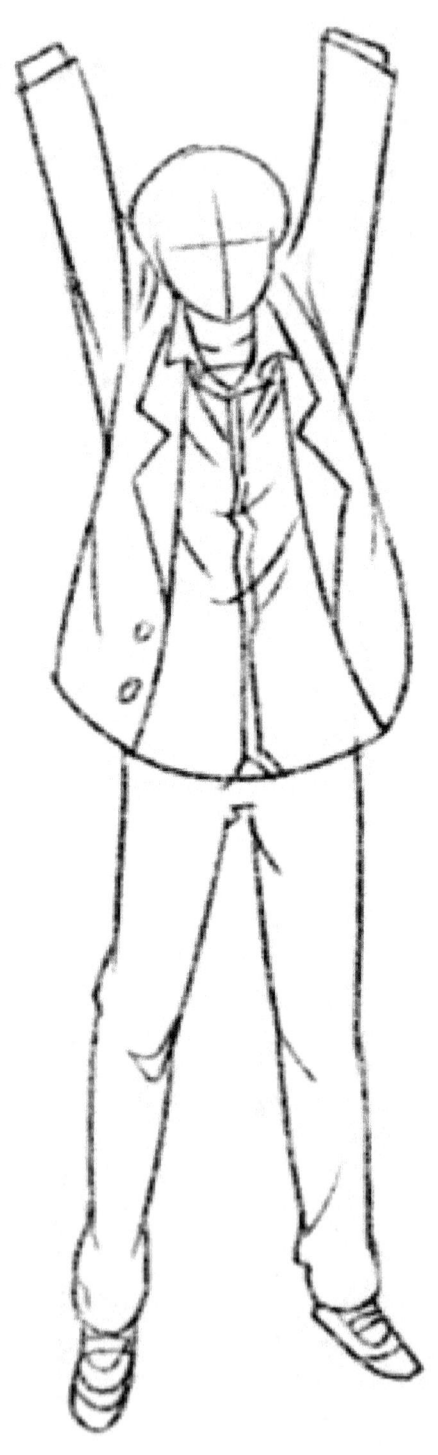

8. Draw hands using square and rectangle shapes:

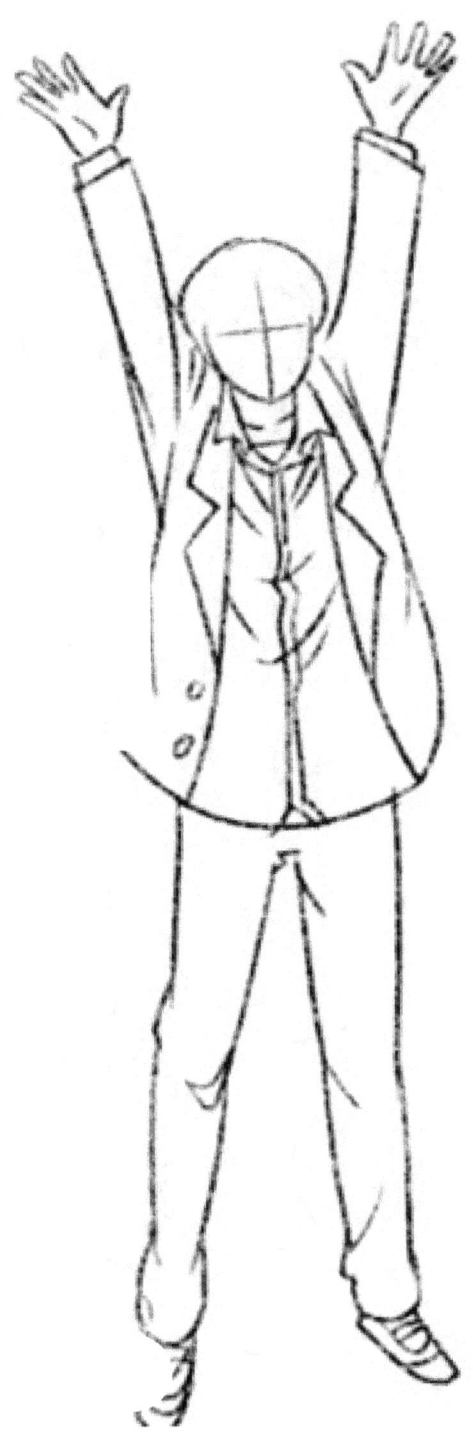

9. Draw hair using jagged lines. Draw facial features:

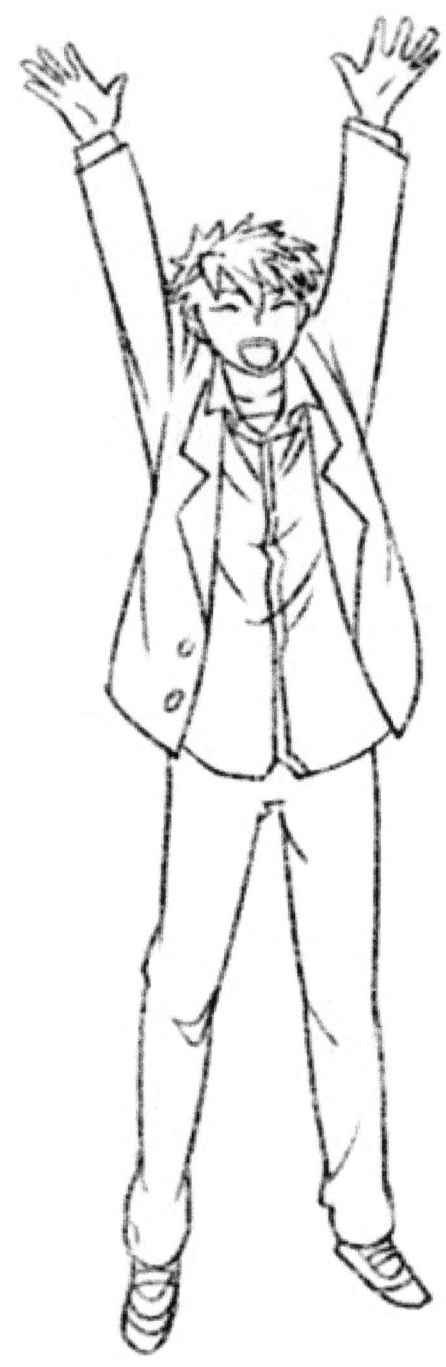

Frustrated Teen Boy

1. Draw a "C" and "V" shape to form the outline of the hair and face:

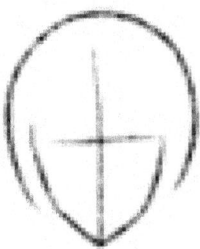

2. Draw a rectangle to create the torso. Draw lines to form the neck:

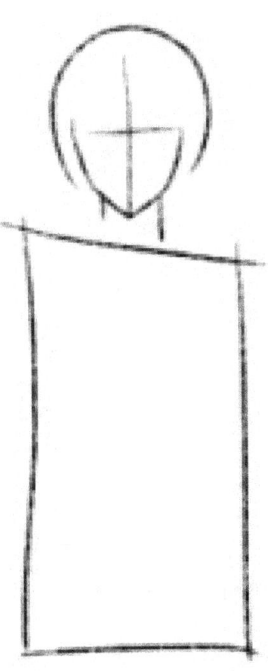

3. Draw lines to outline the legs:

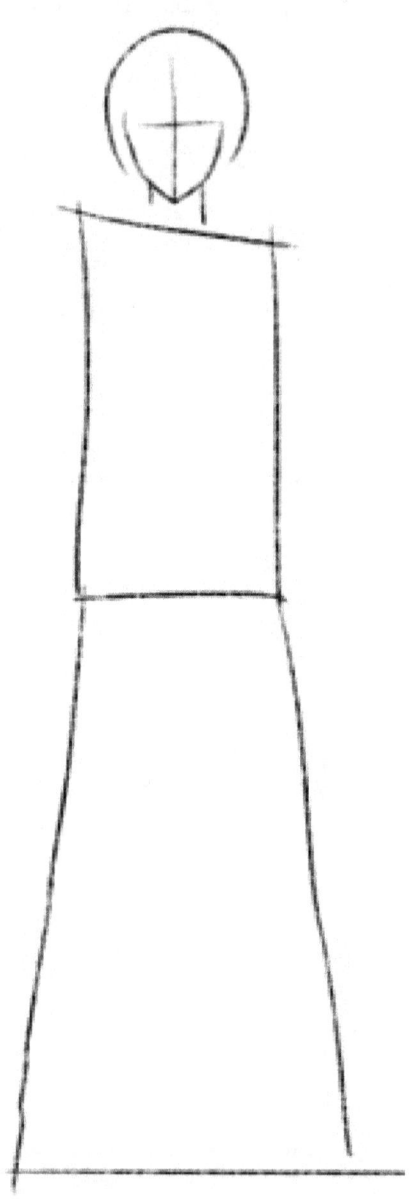

4. Draw rectangles and squares to make the arms and hands:

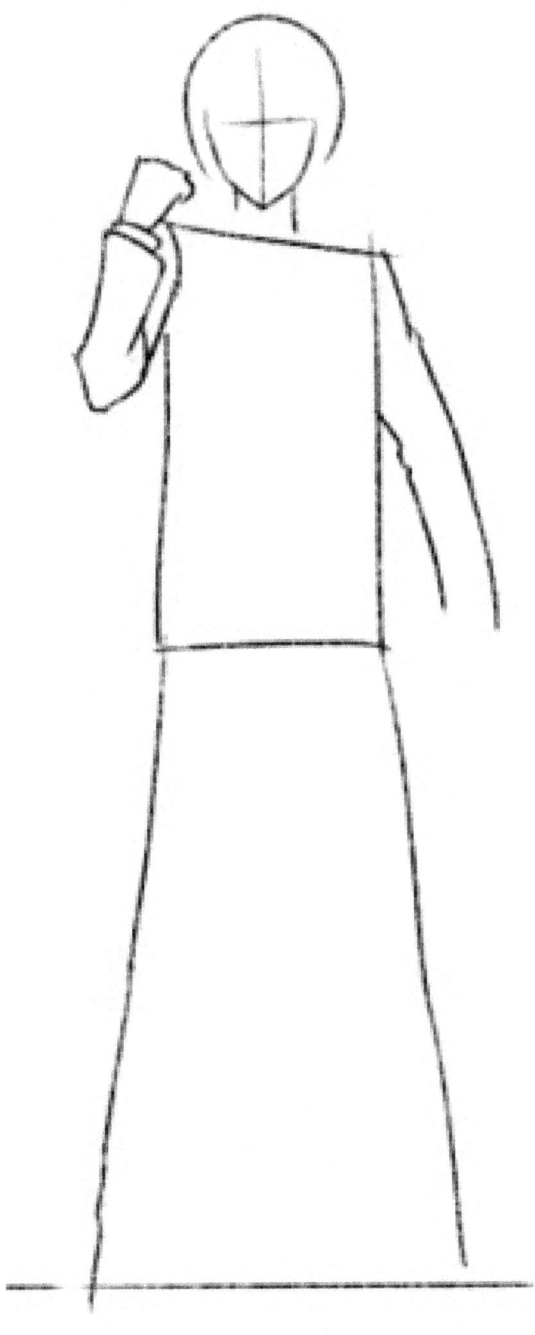

5. Add lines and triangle shapes to detail the clothes:

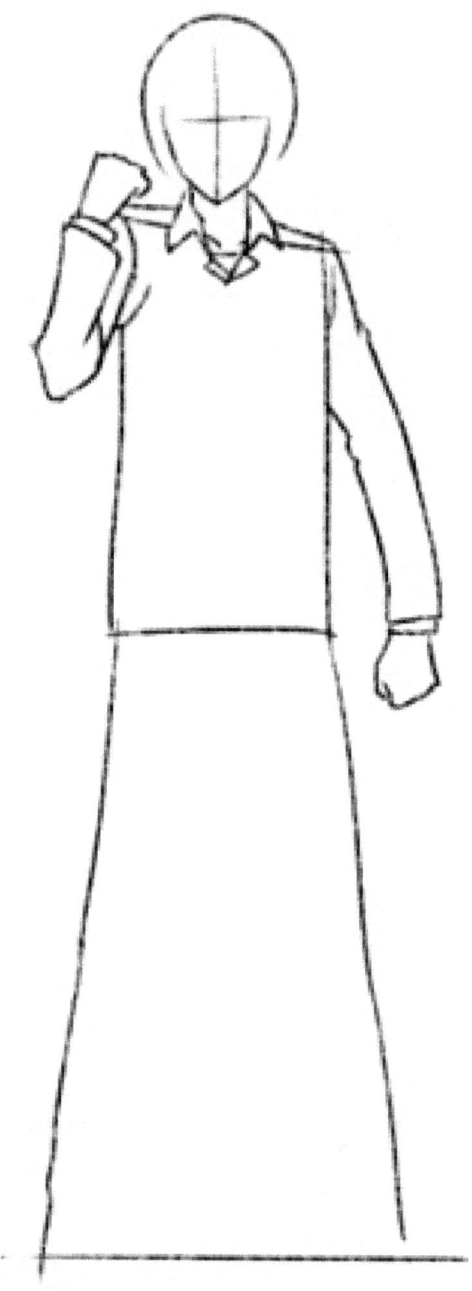

6. Draw more clothing details:

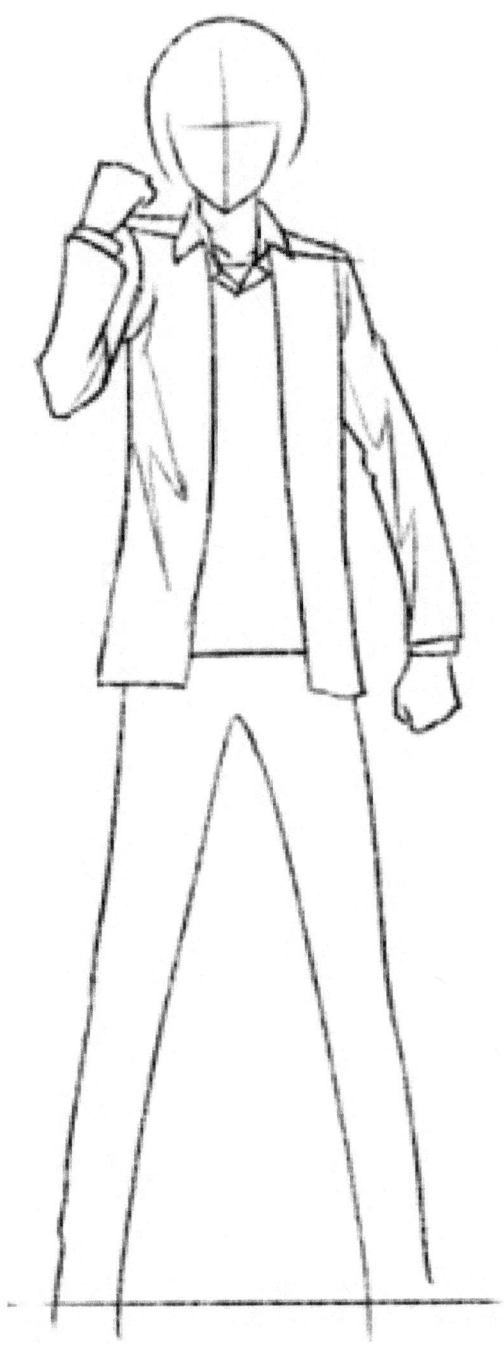

7. Add more slanted lines for clothing wrinkles:

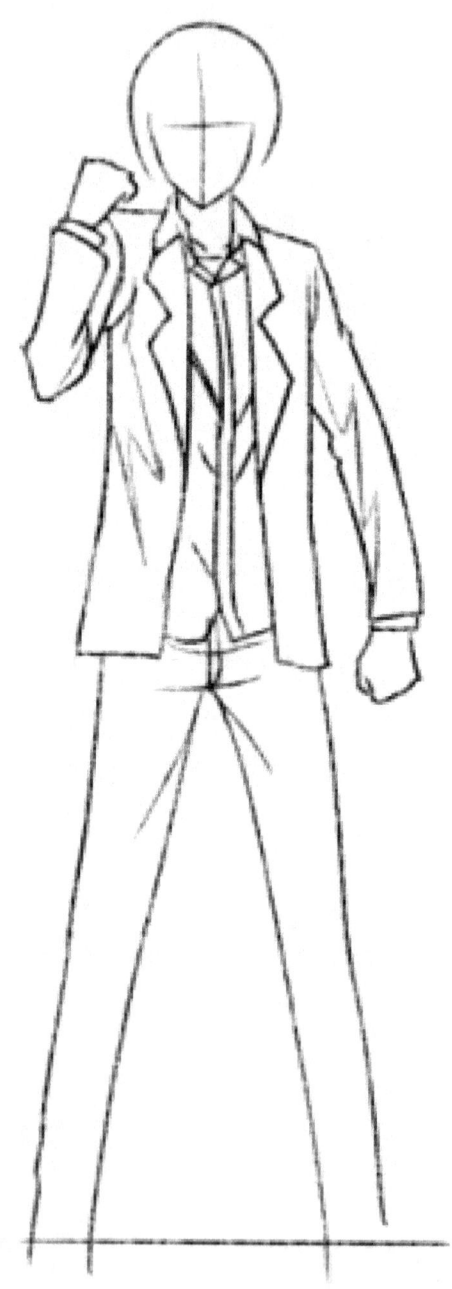

8. Add more clothing details and draw the shoes:

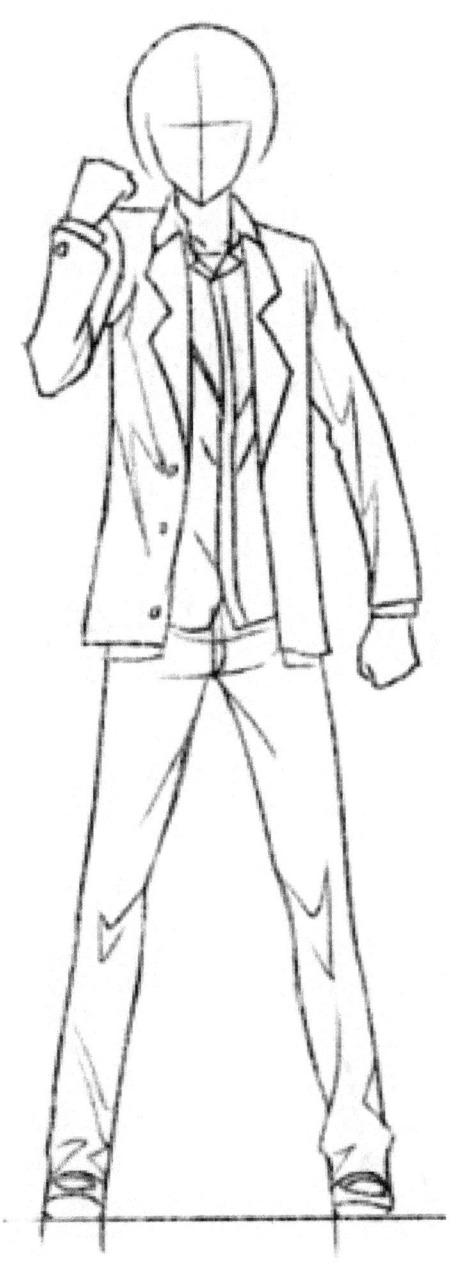

9. Draw facial features:

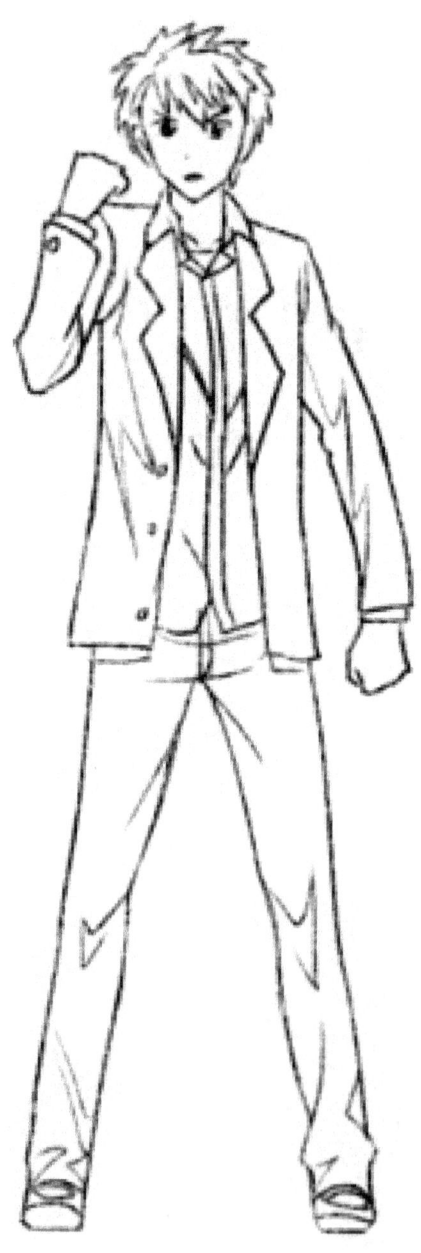

Sparing Teen Boy

1. Draw lines to create the torso:

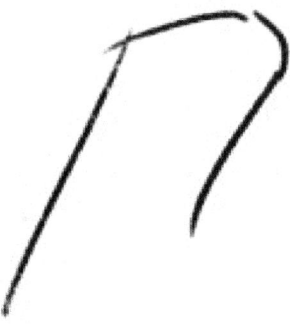

2. Draw rectangle shapes for the legs:

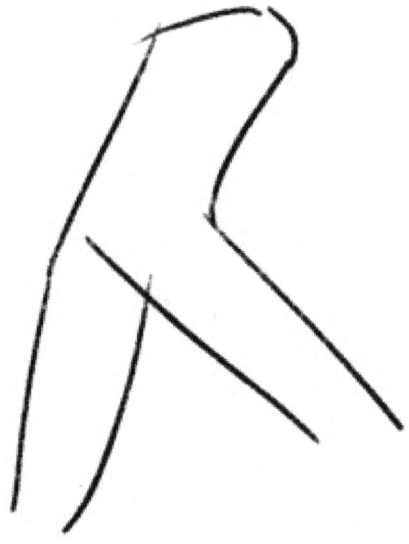

3. Add sharp lines to finish the legs:

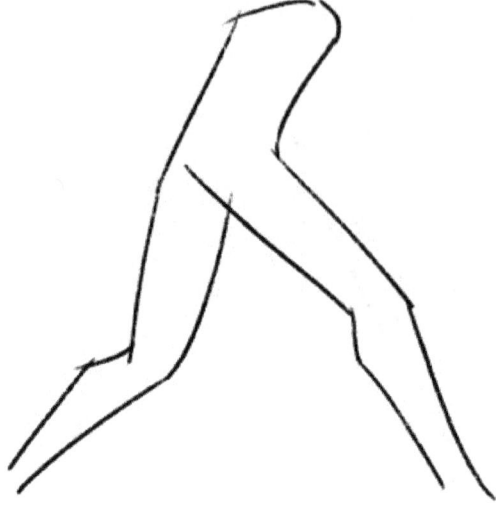

4. Draw a semi-circle for the shoulder. Add rectangle shapes for the right arm:

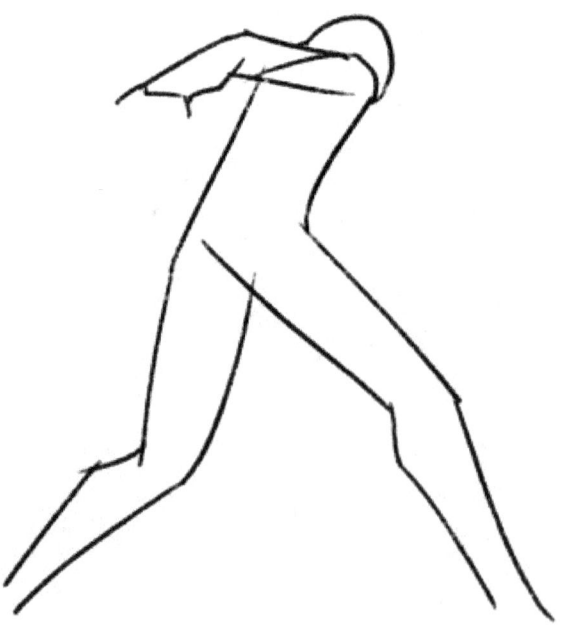

5. Draw a "V" like shape and an arc to create the head:

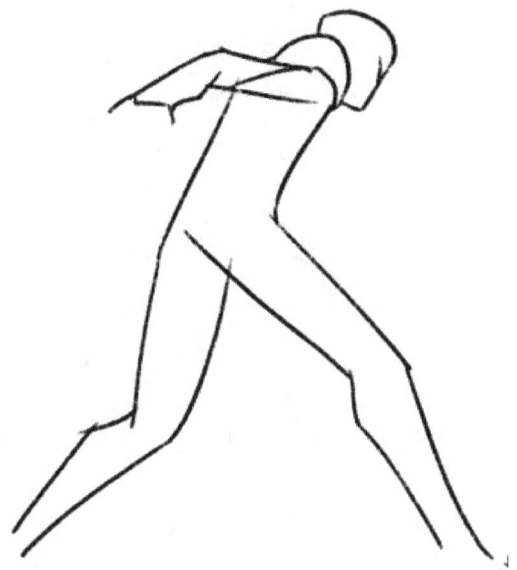

6. Form feet and draw the left hand:

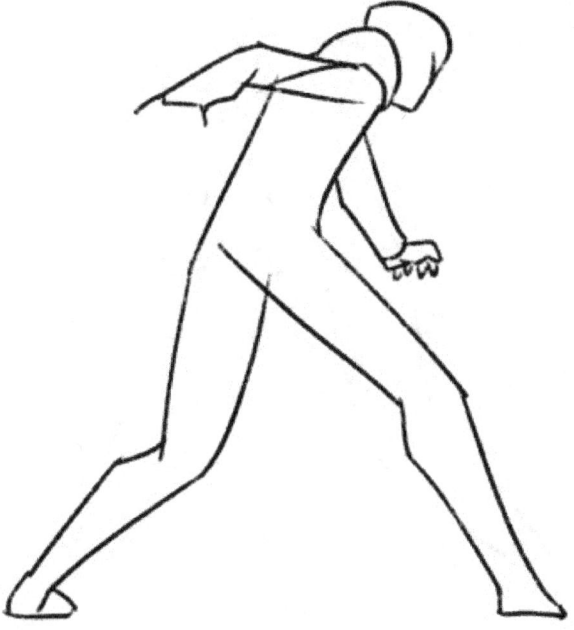

7. Draw the right hand and contour the hair:

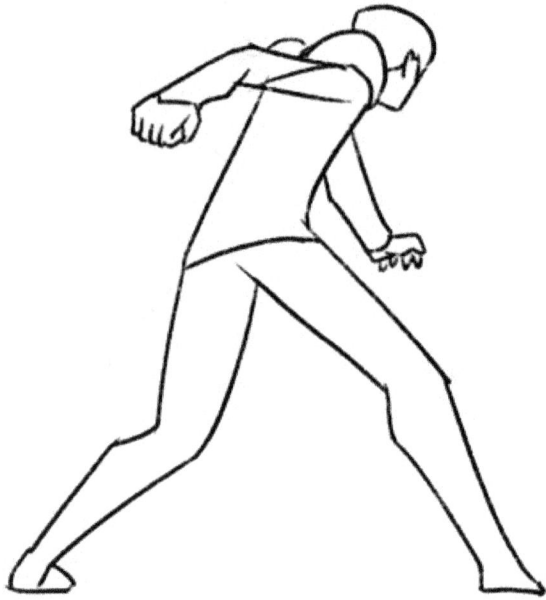

8. Draw wrinkle lines and add lines to create the shoes:

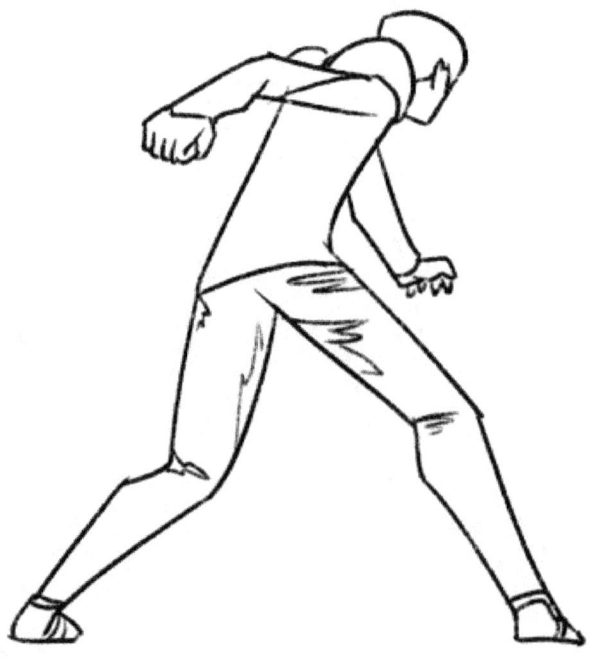

9. Add more wrinkle lines:

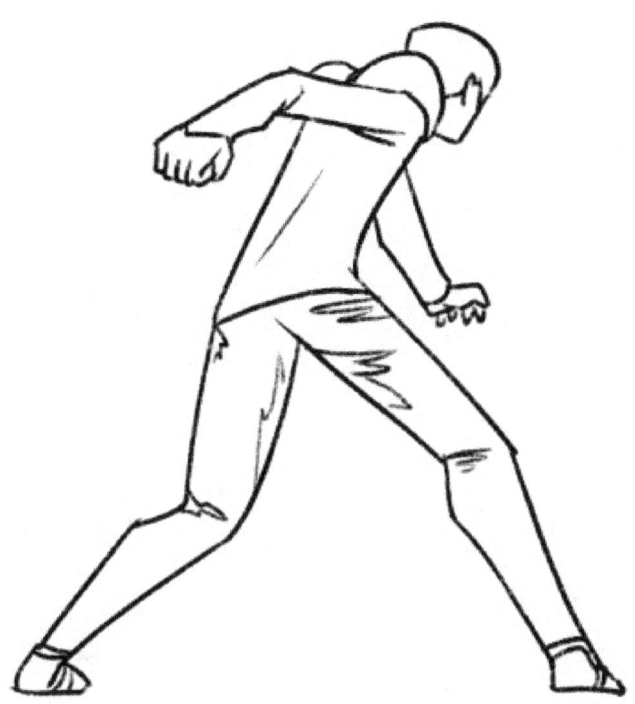

Confident Teen Boy

1. Draw lines to form the jaw line and face:

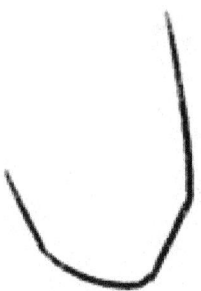

2. Draw small semi-circles for the ear and jagged lines for the hair:

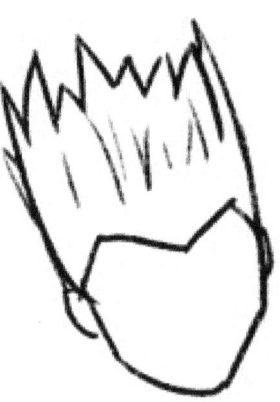

3. Draw line for the shoulders. Draw lines for the arms:

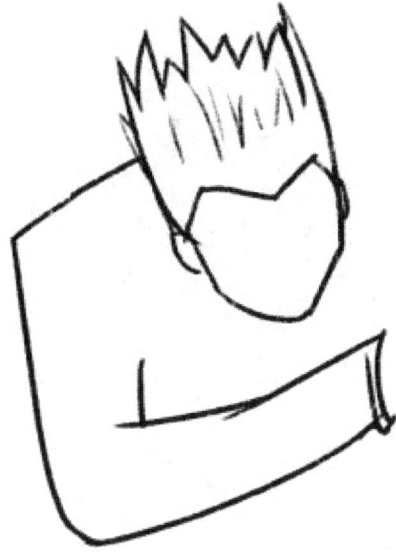

4. Draw arcs to form the right shoulder:

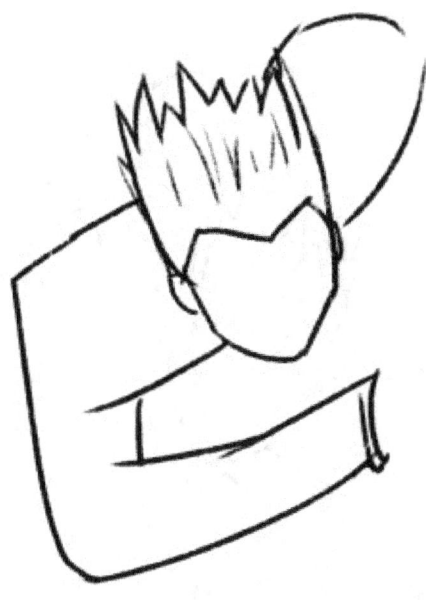

5. Draw triangle and rectangle shapes to make the right arm:

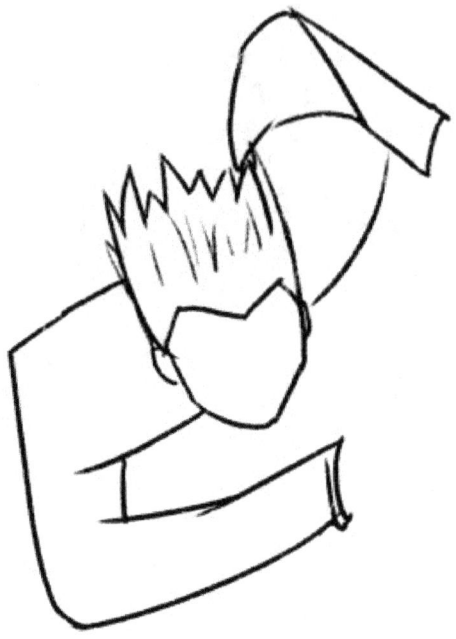

6. Add lines to form the torso and a "U" shape for the leg:

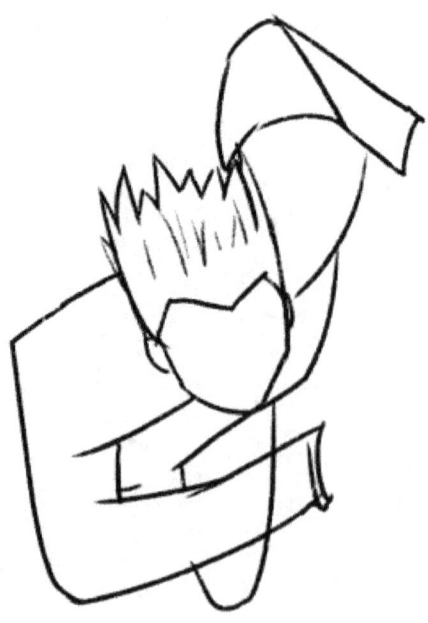

7. Add a series of small arcs to make the foot:

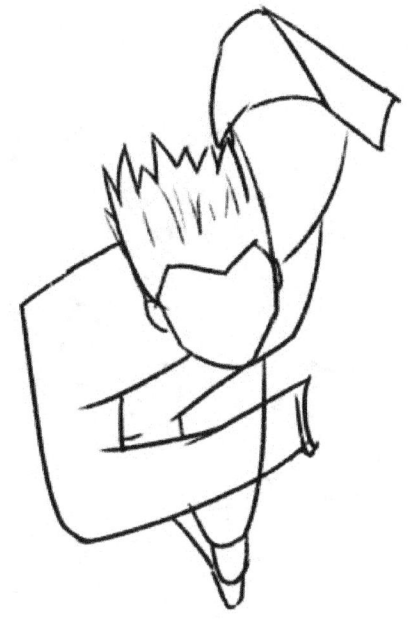

8. Draw hands using rectangle and square shapes:

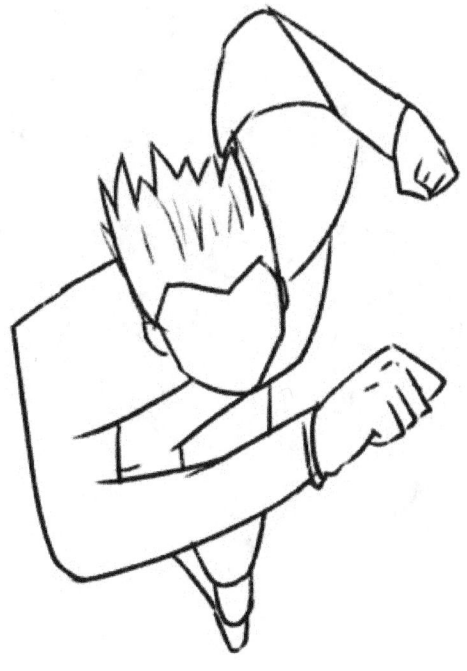

9. Draw lines to outline the facial features:

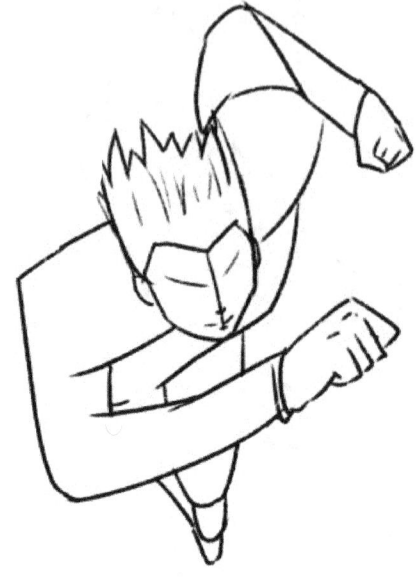

10. Draw almond shapes and circles for the eyes:

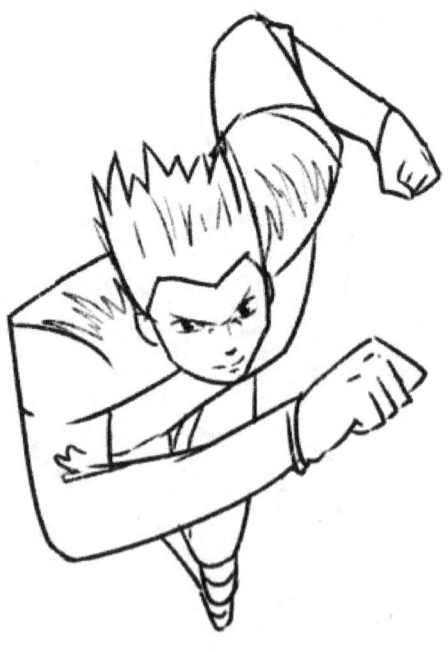

Sword Fighting Teen Boy

1. Draw a "V" shape for the face:

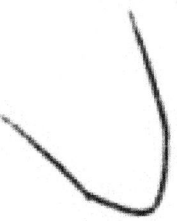

2. Draw lines for shoulders, and a "W" like shape for the hair:

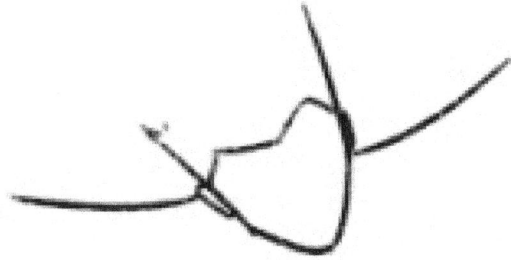

3. Add jagged lines to detail the hair and draw arcs to form the shoulders:

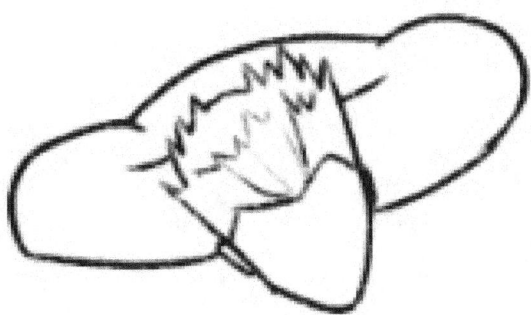

4. Draw rectangle lines for the left leg:

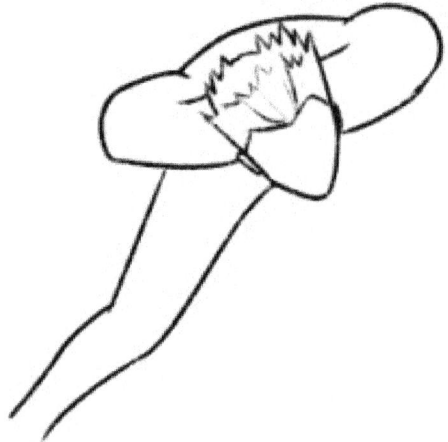

5. Draw rectangle lines to form the right leg:

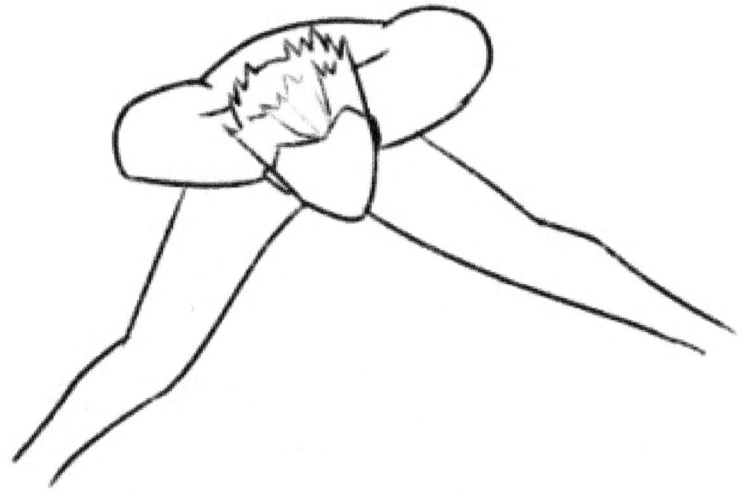

6. Use thin rectangle shapes to create arms:

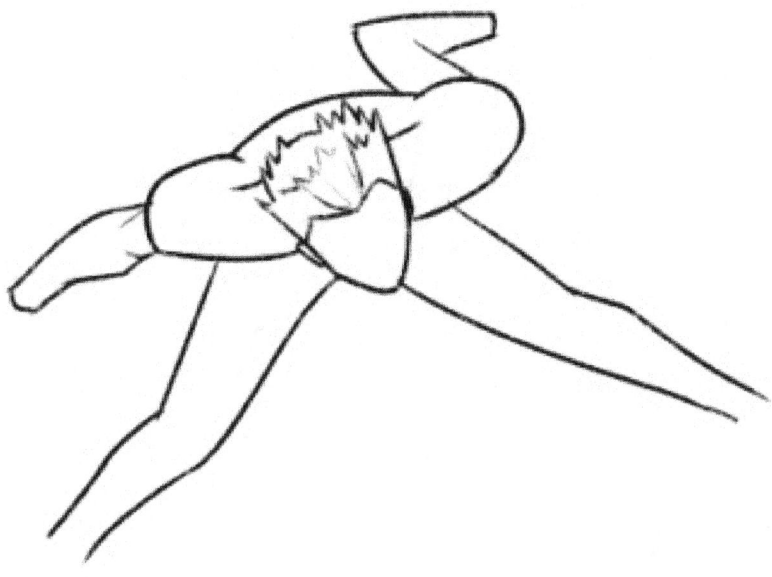

7. Draw hands using square shapes and feet using oval shapes:

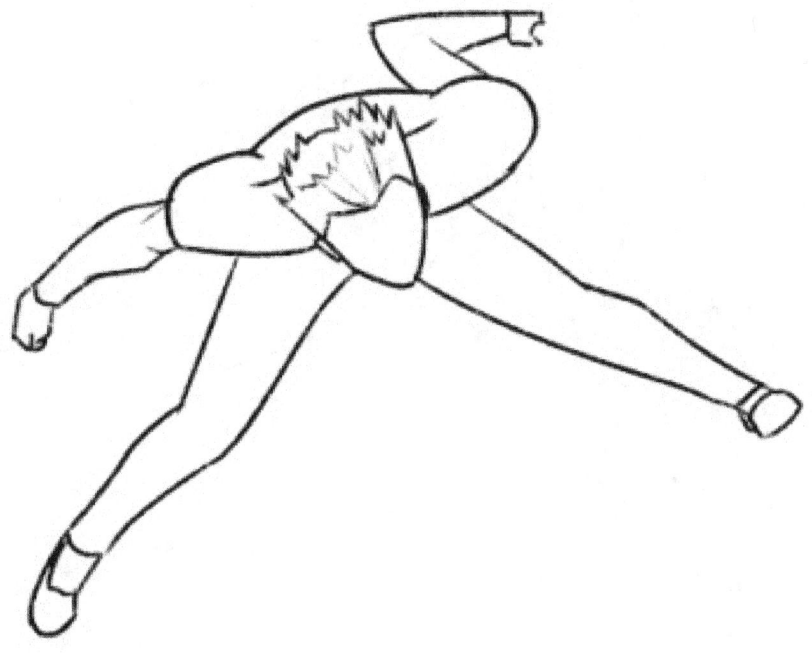

8. Draw the sword using long thin lines:

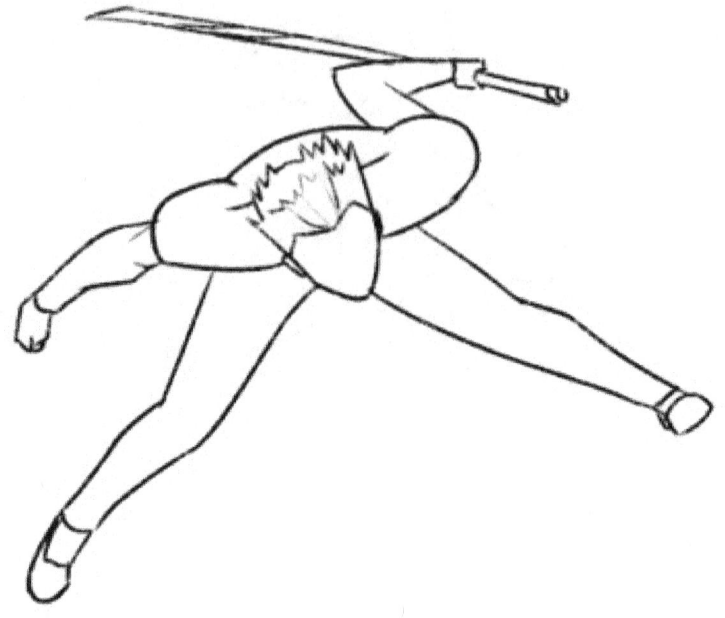

9. Draw lines and dots to create facial features:

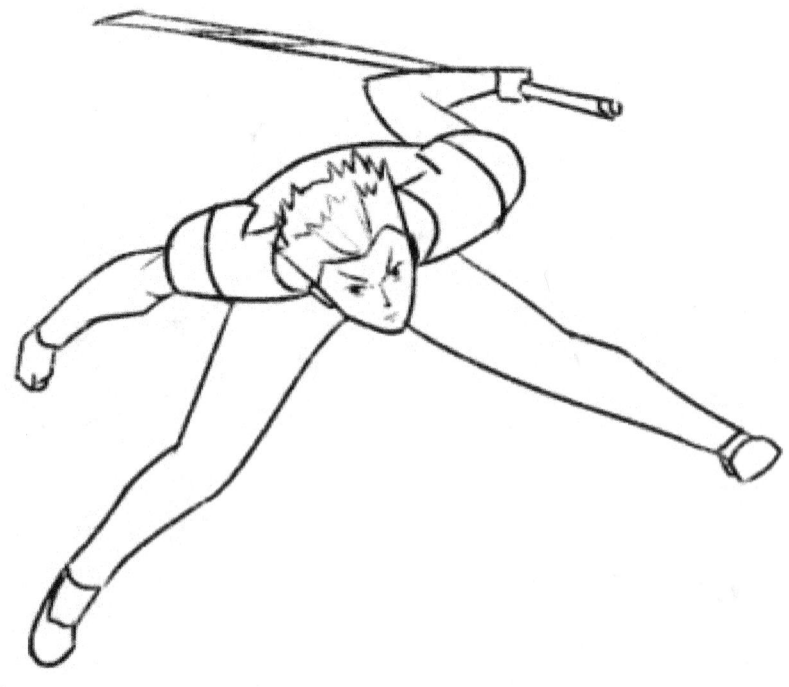

10. Add circles and lines to detail the clothing:

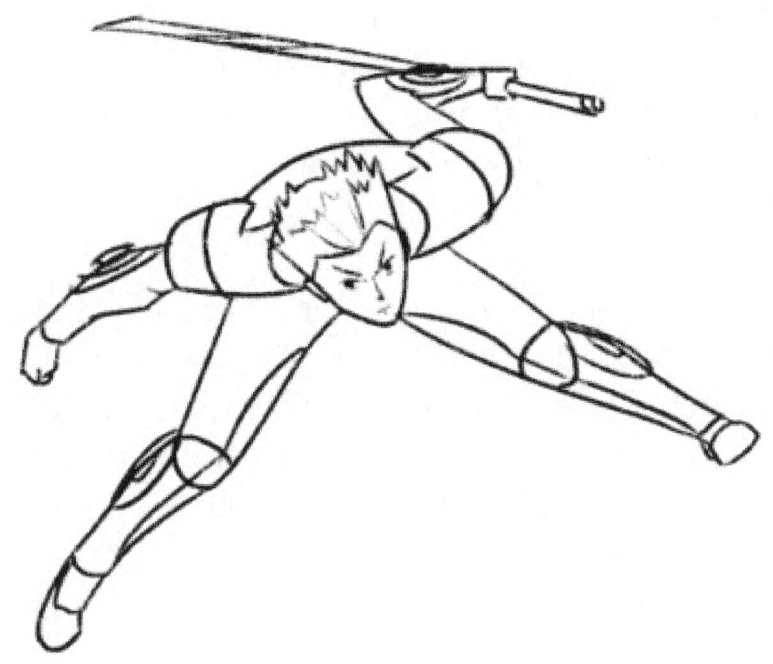

Conclusion

As you may have noticed while drawing these characters, certain gestures were repeated quite often. Anime characters normally have big expressive eyes and small other facial features with little detail. They also typically possess wild, sharp hair and small hands and feet.

If you completed this book, you had practice drawing thirty different characters. And through drawing each one, I'm sure you found it easier and easier to create certain details as your muscles began to memorize the strokes for features like sharp hair and curved faces. Keep practicing, and in time you will be able to draw anime like a pro!

Thank you!

Thank you for choosing our book.

If you liked the book, please leave your feedback on **AMAZON.COM**

We would really appreciate this!

If you would like to have a bonus – **FREE BOOK**, please send the screenshot or the link of your review to this e-mail:

gloria.kemer@gmail.com and we will send you a **FREE BOOK** in PDF as a **GIFT**!**

If you want to receive coloring book, please mention it in your message.

** in the e-mail subject please mention the name of the book you reviewed and the author.

www.ingramcontent.com/pod-product-compliance
Lightning Source LLC
Chambersburg PA
CBHW062350220526
45472CB00008B/1761